DUMPLINGS

OVER 100 RECIPES FROM THE HEART OF CHINA TO THE COASTS OF ITALY

Dumplings: Over 100 Recipes from the Heart of China to the Coasts of Italy

13-Digit ISBN: 978-1-60433-900-0
10-Digit ISBN: 1-60433-900-4

This book may be ordered by mail from the publisher. Please include $5.99 for postage and handling. Please support your local bookseller first!

Books published by Cider Mill Press Book Publishers are available at special discounts for bulk purchases in the United States by corporations, institutions, and other organizations. For more information, please contact the publisher.

Cider Mill Press Book Publishers
"Where good books are ready for press"
501 Nelson Place
Nashville, Tennessee 37214

cidermillpress.com

Typography: Bushcraft, Adobe Garamond, Clarendon, Fenway Park, Sentinel Black, Helvetica Round, Neutraface 2

Image Credits: Images on 29, 33, 38, 110, 138, 141, 147, 149, 151, 158, 170, 181, 182, 185, 193, 195, 197, 203, 208 courtesy of Derek Bissonnette. Images on 10, 13, 14, 18, 71, 75, 113, 189, 190, 211, 215 courtesy of Cider Mill Press. All other images used under official license from Shutterstock.com.

Printed in Malaysia

23 24 25 26 27 COS 6 5 4 3 2

DUMPLINGS

OVER 100 RECIPES FROM THE HEART OF CHINA TO THE COASTS OF ITALY

DEREK
BISSONNETTE

CIDER MILL PRESS
BOOK PUBLISHERS

Contents

Introduction

Dumplings: so easy to eat, so difficult to categorize. Used to describe morsels of dough that are simmered in liquid, as well as doughs that encase a delicious filling, few can find common ground when outlining what is, and what is not, a dumpling. For some, pillowy gnocchi and the irresistibly chewy spätzle are the true heirs to the dumpling throne. For many others, the key components of numerous Asian cuisines, like wontons, potstickers, and gyoza, are the rightful rulers. And there are still further divisions within those camps, as some readily welcome pockets like empanadas and Cornish pasties to the dumpling fold, while other folks won't even give them a chance.

While there's considerable debate over what exactly makes up a dumpling, there can be no argument that each and every candidate is delicious. As flavor is always paramount, these recipes are inclined toward the more permissive side of the dumpling debate, letting flavor, instead of some purist's arbitrary demarcation, be the guiding principle.

What this liberal stance opens up is an entire world of flavors. Almost every one of the world's cuisines has some form of dumpling that has become a treasured treat, and when one drills down and takes a look at the essentials, it is easy to see why. Consisting of a simple dough that provides a solid foundation for delightful fillings, rich sauces, and comforting broths, and which can be boiled, pan-fried, deep-fried, or steamed, dumplings' ability to combine flavors and textures and turn odds and ends into exceptional innovations make them an ideal concern for the economical epicure.

With a comforting and unpretentious air that is reminiscent of home, dumplings reward patience, preparation, attention to detail, and ingenuity. As you'll see while working your way through the preparations in this book, part of what makes them so difficult to define is that they are as closely associated with the feelings they inspire as they are with the cuisines and techniques that brought them to life.

Cover Your Bases

Almost all of your dalliances with dumplings will start with one of the recipes in this chapter. Whether you want something other than the standard noodle to go with the sauce you're making, got carried away by the beauty and bounty at the farmers market and need to contain all that produce, or are in need of comfort now that bad weather washed away your weekend plans, the dumpling doughs, batters, and wrappers in this chapter are where you'll want to turn.

Potato Gnocchi

YIELD: 8 SERVINGS • ACTIVE TIME: 1 HOUR • TOTAL TIME: 2½ HOURS

This nubby, ridged pasta may be the best-known dumpling of all, thanks to a neutral flavor that makes it extremely versatile.

INGREDIENTS

3 lbs. Yukon Gold potatoes

2 large eggs

2½ cups all-purpose flour, plus more for dusting

1 tablespoon kosher salt

1 Preheat the oven to 400°F. Place the potatoes on a baking sheet, prick them several times with a fork, and bake until they are soft all the way through, about 1 hour. Remove from oven, slice them open, and let cool completely.

2 When the potatoes are cool enough to handle, scoop the flesh into a mixing bowl and mash until smooth. Make a well in the center of the potatoes and add the eggs, 1½ cups of the flour, and the salt. Work the mixture with your hands to combine, and then add the remaining flour in small increments. Knead the dough to incorporate and stop adding flour as soon as the dough holds together and is no longer sticky.

3 Place a handful of dough on a flour-dusted work surface and roll it into a ¾" thick rope with your hands. Repeat with the remaining dough.

4 Cut the ropes into ½" pieces and roll the gnocchi over the tines of a fork (or a gnocchi board) while gently pressing down to create ridges. If the gnocchi start sticking to the fork, dip it into flour before pressing the gnocchi against it. Place the shaped gnocchi on a parchment-lined baking sheet and lightly dust with flour. If not cooking immediately, cover and refrigerate for up to 1 day or freeze for up to 3 months. To cook the gnocchi, follow the instructions in Step 2 on page 66.

Sweet Potato Gnocchi

YIELD: 6 SERVINGS • ACTIVE TIME: 1 HOUR • TOTAL TIME: 2½ HOURS

By utilizing sweet potatoes and ricotta, this version captures the feeling of fall and still carries the lightness that makes gnocchi so wonderful.

INGREDIENTS

2½ lbs. sweet potatoes

½ cup ricotta cheese

1 egg

2 egg yolks

1 tablespoon kosher salt, plus more to taste

1 teaspoon pepper

3 tablespoons light brown sugar

2 tablespoons maple syrup

2 cups all-purpose flour, plus more as needed

1 cup semolina flour

1 Preheat the oven to 400°F. Wash the sweet potatoes, place them on a parchment-lined baking sheet, and use a knife to pierce several holes in the tops of the potatoes. Place in the oven and cook until they are soft all the way through, 45 minutes to 1 hour. Remove from the oven, slice them open, and let cool completely.

2 Scrape the cooled sweet potato flesh into a mixing bowl and mash until smooth. Add the ricotta, egg, egg yolks, salt, pepper, brown sugar, and maple syrup and stir until thoroughly combined. Add the flours 1 cup at a time and work the mixture with your hands until the dough holds together and is no longer sticky. If it is too moist, add all-purpose flour in 1-teaspoon increments until it ceases to be sticky.

3 Transfer the dough to a lightly floured work surface and cut into 10 even pieces. Roll each piece into a long rope, cut the ropes into ½" pieces, and roll the gnocchi over the tines of a fork (or a gnocchi board) while gently pressing down to create ridges. Place the shaped dumplings on a parchment-lined baking sheet, and lightly dust with flour. If not cooking immediately, cover and refrigerate for up to 1 day or freeze for up to 3 months. To cook the gnocchi, follow the instructions in Step 1 on page 70.

14 Cover Your Bases

Arugula & Boursin Gnocchi

YIELD: 6 SERVINGS • ACTIVE TIME: 1 HOUR • TOTAL TIME: 2½ HOURS

A little butter and a bit of shaved truffle are the only accessories these flavor-packed pillows require.

INGREDIENTS

- ½ lb. arugula, stems removed
- 1½ lbs. Yukon Gold potatoes
- 1 large egg
- 2 tablespoons extra virgin olive oil
- 1⅔ cups all-purpose flour, plus more for dusting
- ¼ cup grated Parmesan cheese
- 3 tablespoons Boursin cheese
- 2 teaspoons kosher salt
- White pepper, to taste

1 Preheat the oven to 400°F. Place a 10" skillet on the stove and turn the heat to medium-high. Add the arugula and cook until the leaves have softened but are still bright green. Transfer to a colander to cool. When cool enough to handle, squeeze any remaining water out of the arugula and mince. Set aside.

2 Place the potatoes on a baking sheet, prick them several times with a fork, and bake until they are soft all the way through, about 1 hour. Remove from oven, slice them open, and let cool completely. As the potatoes cool, place the arugula, egg, and olive oil in a food processor and pulse until smooth. When the potatoes are cool enough to handle, scoop the flesh into a mixing bowl and mash until smooth. Add the arugula mixture, flour, cheeses, salt, and white pepper and work the mixture with your hands until the dough holds together.

3 Place the dough on a floured work surface and knead until soft and smooth, about 5 minutes. Cut the dough into eight pieces and roll each one into a ¾" thick rope with your hands. Cut the ropes into ½" pieces and roll the gnocchi over the tines of a fork (or a gnocchi board) while gently pressing down to create ridges. Place the shaped gnocchi on a parchment-lined baking sheet and lightly dust with flour. If not cooking immediately, cover and refrigerate for up to 1 day or freeze for up to 3 weeks. To cook the gnocchi, follow the instructions in Step 2 on page 73.

Baccalà Gnocchi

YIELD: 8 SERVINGS • ACTIVE TIME: 1½ HOURS • TOTAL TIME: 3 DAYS

If you have the ability to plan ahead, the baccalà adds an irresistible chewiness to gnocchi.

INGREDIENTS

5 oz. baccalà (dried, salted cod)

1⅓ lbs. Yukon Gold potatoes

⅓ cup grated Manchego cheese

Zest of 1 lemon

¾ cup all-purpose flour, plus more as needed

1 large egg, beaten

Salt and white pepper, to taste

1 Three days before you intend to make the gnocchi, place the baccalà in a large baking dish and cover with water. Cover with plastic wrap and refrigerate for 3 days, while changing the water twice a day. After 3 days, drain the baccalà, remove any remaining skin or bones, pat dry with paper towels, and mince. Set aside.

2 Preheat the oven to 400°F. Place the potatoes on a baking sheet, prick them several times with a fork, and bake until they are soft all the way through, about 1 hour. Remove from oven, slice them open, and let them cool. When cool enough to handle, scoop the flesh into a large mixing bowl and mash until smooth.

3 Sprinkle the cheese, lemon zest, ⅓ cup of the baccalà, the flour, egg, salt, and white pepper over the potatoes. Use a bench scraper to work the mixture until the dough holds together, is no longer sticky, and is homogenous. If the dough is too moist, incorporate more flour as needed. Shape the dough into a square block and lightly flour a work surface. Cut off a 1" slice of the dough, roll it into a long ½" thick rope, and cut into ½" pieces. Roll the gnocchi over the tines of a fork (or a gnocchi board) while gently pressing down to create ridges. Place the shaped gnocchi on a parchment-lined baking sheet and lightly dust with flour. If not cooking immediately, cover and refrigerate for up to 1 day or freeze for up to 3 weeks. To cook the gnocchi, follow the instructions in Step 2 on page 74.

Chocolate & Cheese Gnocchi

YIELD: 8 SERVINGS • ACTIVE TIME: 45 MINUTES • TOTAL TIME: 2 HOURS

You may think these dumplings are sweet, but the cocoa powder and sugar are only here to further amplify the savory side.

INGREDIENTS

1½ lbs. Yukon Gold potatoes

1¾ cups all-purpose flour, plus more as needed

2 tablespoons unsweetened cocoa powder

2 teaspoons sugar

½ teaspoon ground cinnamon

5 oz. Brie cheese, at room temperature, rind removed

2 large eggs, lightly beaten

1 tablespoon kosher salt, plus more to taste

White pepper, to taste

1 Preheat the oven to 400°F. Place the potatoes on a baking sheet, prick them several times with a fork, and bake until they are soft all the way through, about 1 hour. Remove from oven, slice them open, and let cool completely.

2 When the potatoes are cool enough to handle, scoop the flesh into a mixing bowl and mash until smooth. Add the flour, cocoa powder, sugar, cinnamon, Brie, eggs, salt, and white pepper and work the mixture with your hands until the dough holds together. Knead the dough until it is smooth, about 5 minutes. To test the dough, bring a small saucepan of water to a boil. Drop in a small ball of dough and wait until it floats to the surface, which should take no longer than 2 minutes. If the ball falls apart or has a soft, mushy texture, incorporate flour in 1-tablespoon increments until the desired texture has been achieved.

3 Cut the dough into 10 equal pieces and roll each piece into a long ½" thick rope. Cut each into ½" pieces and roll the gnocchi over the tines of a fork (or a gnocchi board) while gently pressing down to create ridges. Place the shaped gnocchi on a parchment-lined baking sheet and lightly dust with flour. If not cooking immediately, cover and refrigerate for up to 1 day or freeze for up to 3 weeks. To cook, follow the instructions in Step 2 on page 77.

Chickpea Gnocchi

YIELD: 4 SERVINGS • ACTIVE TIME: 1 HOUR • TOTAL TIME: 1 HOUR

Light and nutty, these dumplings are perfect when you need a fix in the middle of summer.

INGREDIENTS

1 (14 oz.) can of chickpeas

4 large egg yolks

1 tablespoon water

1½ cups all-purpose flour, plus more for dusting

1½ teaspoons kosher salt, plus more to taste

1 Drain the chickpeas and rinse them well under cold water. Using your thumb and index finger, remove the outer skin from each chickpea. Place the chickpeas, egg yolks, and water in a food processor and puree until smooth. Transfer the puree to a mixing bowl and add the flour and salt. Knead until a soft, tacky dough forms, about 8 minutes. The dough should have no elasticity whatsoever. If you poke it with a finger, the indentation should remain.

2 Lightly dust a work surface with flour. Tear off a handful of the dough and cover the rest with clear food wrap to keep it from drying out. Roll the dough into a long rope about ½" thick and cut into ½" pieces. Roll the gnocchi over the tines of a fork (or a gnocchi board) while gently pressing down to create ridges. If the gnocchi start sticking to the fork, dip it into flour before pressing the gnocchi against it. Place the shaped gnocchi on a parchment-lined baking sheet and lightly dust with flour. Repeat with the remaining dough. If not cooking immediately, cover and refrigerate for up to 1 day or freeze for up to 3 weeks. To cook the dumplings, follow the instructions in Step 3 on page 78.

Canederli

YIELD: 4 TO 6 SERVINGS • ACTIVE TIME: 40 MINUTES • TOTAL TIME: 1 HOUR

These plump bread dumplings hail from the heavily Austrian-influenced Trentino-Alto Adige region in northern Italy.

INGREDIENTS

1½ tablespoons unsalted butter

1 yellow onion, minced

Salt and pepper, to taste

3 large eggs

1 cup whole milk

¼ cup minced parsley leaves

½ lb. day-old crusty bread, crusts removed, cut into small cubes

¾ cup all-purpose flour, plus more as needed

1 Warm a large skillet over medium-low heat for 2 to 3 minutes. Add the butter and raise the heat to medium. When the butter has melted and stopped foaming, add the onion and a couple pinches of salt and stir to incorporate. When the onion starts to sizzle, reduce heat to low, cover, and cook, while stirring occasionally, until the onion is very soft, about 20 minutes. Remove from heat and set aside.

2 Place the eggs and milk in a large bowl and whisk to combine. Add the onion, parsley, and pieces of bread and work the mixture with your hands until the bread starts to break down. Add the flour and use your hands to work the mixture until it starts to hold together as a slightly tacky dough. If it doesn't stick together, incorporate additional flour, 1 tablespoon at a time.

3 Pinch off a piece of dough large enough to roll into a ball that is the size of a walnut. Form the dough into a ball, roll on a flour-dusted work surface, and place on a parchment-lined baking sheet. Repeat with the remaining dough. If not cooking immediately, cover the canederli with plastic wrap and store in the refrigerator for up to 2 days. To cook the canederli, follow the instructions in Step 2 on page 81.

Passatelli

YIELD: 8 SERVINGS • ACTIVE TIME: 20 MINUTES • TOTAL TIME: 2½ HOURS

Their name means "to be passed through," alluding to the act of pushing the dough through a spätzle maker.

INGREDIENTS

- 1¼ cups very fine bread crumbs, plus more as needed
- 1¼ cups grated Parmesan cheese
- 2 tablespoons unsalted butter, melted
- 1 handful of fresh parsley leaves, minced
- 3 large eggs, plus more as needed
- 1 teaspoon grated nutmeg or lemon zest
- 1 teaspoon kosher salt, plus more to taste
- ½ teaspoon white pepper

1 Place all of the ingredients in a large mixing bowl. Work the mixture with your hands until a firm, slightly sticky dough forms. If the mixture feels too wet, incorporate more bread crumbs, 1 tablespoon at a time. Cover the dough with plastic wrap and let rest at room temperature for 15 minutes.

2 Bring water to a boil in a small saucepan. Form a pinch of dough into a ball and drop it in the water. If it falls apart, add another egg to the dough and stir to incorporate. Working in batches, place handfuls of dough into the cup of a spätzle maker that has been greased with nonstick cooking spray. Press down to squeeze long ropes of dough out the other side. Cut the ropes into 1½" pieces and transfer them to a parchment-lined baking sheet. Let dry for 1½ hours.

3 To cook the passatelli, bring a large pot of salted water to a boil. Reduce heat to a gentle boil and add the passatelli. After they float to the surface, about 4 minutes, let them cook for a minute longer. Remove and add to a broth or your preferred sauce.

NOTE: SPÄTZLE MAKERS ARE REASONABLY PRICED, ABOUT $7 FOR A SERVICEABLE ONE. IF YOU DO NOT HAVE ONE, YOU CAN USE A BOX GRATER OR CUT THE DOUGH INTO SLICES THAT ARE ⅛" THICK AND 2" LONG.

Spätzle

YIELD: 6 SERVINGS • ACTIVE TIME: 30 MINUTES • TOTAL TIME: 1½ HOURS

Meaning "little sparrows" in German, spätzle are fantastic alongside braised or roasted meats, particularly when tossed with the juices.

INGREDIENTS

2½ cups all-purpose flour

1 tablespoon kosher salt, plus more to taste

2 large eggs

1¼ cups whole milk, plus more as needed

1 Place the flour, salt, eggs, and milk in a mixing bowl and stir until the dough becomes somewhat shiny and resembles pancake batter, 7 to 8 minutes. If the dough seems too thick, incorporate more milk, 1 teaspoon at a time. Cover the bowl with plastic wrap and let rest at room temperature for 1 hour.

2 Bring a large pot of salted water to a boil and prepare an ice water bath. Reduce the heat so the water is gently boiling. Working in batches, place handfuls of dough into the cup of a spätzle maker that has been greased with nonstick cooking spray. While pressing down, grate the dough into the boiling water and cook until the spätzle float to the top. Stir occasionally to prevent the spätzle from sticking to the bottom. Remove the cooked spätzle with a slotted spoon and transfer them to the ice water bath. When all of the spätzle are cooked, place them on paper towels to dry. When dry, serve with your favorite sauce, sauté in butter, or serve alongside a braised or roasted meat.

Sweet Potato Spätzle

YIELD: 6 TO 8 SERVINGS • ACTIVE TIME: 45 MINUTES • TOTAL TIME: 2 HOURS

The sweet potato can be replaced by pumpkin, or any other member of the squash family.

INGREDIENTS

3 lbs. sweet potatoes

1 cup all-purpose flour

1 teaspoon kosher salt, plus more to taste

2 eggs, separated into yolks and whites

1 Preheat the oven to 400°F. Place the sweet potatoes on a baking sheet, prick them several times with a fork, and bake until they are soft all the way through, about 1 hour. Remove from oven, slice them open, and let cool completely.

2 When the sweet potatoes are cool enough to handle, scoop the flesh into a food processor and puree until smooth. Place the sweet potato puree in a saucepan and cook, while stirring frequently, over low heat until the puree has reduced to 2 cups, about 30 minutes. This will help concentrate the flavor. Transfer the reduced puree to a mixing bowl and let cool for 10 minutes.

3 Bring a pot of salted water to a boil and prepare an ice water bath. Add the flour and salt to the puree and fold to incorporate. Add the egg yolks and whisk to combine. Place the egg whites in a separate bowl and beat until soft peaks form. Fold the beaten egg whites into the sweet potato mixture.

4 Working in batches, place handfuls of dough into the cup of a spätzle maker that has been greased with nonstick cooking spray. While pressing down, grate the dough into the boiling water and cook until the spätzle float to the top. Stir occasionally to prevent the spätzle from sticking to the bottom. Remove the cooked spätzle with a slotted spoon and transfer them to the ice water bath. When all of the spätzle are cooked, place them on paper towels to dry. When dry, serve with your favorite sauce or sauté in butter.

Chard Spätzle

YIELD: 4 SERVINGS • ACTIVE TIME: 1 HOUR • TOTAL TIME: 2 HOURS

A wonderful place to start if you're intrigued, and a little intimidated, by making pasta at home.

INGREDIENTS

1½ tablespoons kosher salt, plus more to taste

2 lbs. Swiss chard, stems removed

4 large eggs

1 teaspoon grated nutmeg

2 cups all-purpose flour, plus more as needed

¼ cup water

Milk, at room temperature, as needed

1 Bring a large pot of salted water to a boil. Add the chard and cook until wilted, about 3 minutes. Drain the chard and rinse under cold water. Drain well and squeeze to remove as much liquid as possible. Transfer to a clean kitchen towel and pat dry.

2 Place the chard, eggs, nutmeg, and 1½ tablespoons salt in a food processor and pulse until the greens are mostly shredded. Add the flour and water and puree until the mixture is smooth, stopping to scrape down the work bowl as needed. Transfer the dough to a mixing bowl. The dough should resemble pancake batter. If it seems too thick, incorporate the milk, 1 teaspoon at a time. Cover with plastic wrap and let sit for 1 hour.

3 Bring a large pot of salted water to a boil and prepare an ice water bath. Reduce the heat so the water is gently boiling. Working in batches, place handfuls of dough into the cup of a spätzle maker that has been greased with nonstick cooking spray. While pressing down, grate the dough into the boiling water and cook until the spätzle float to the top. Stir occasionally to prevent the spätzle from sticking to the bottom. Remove the cooked spätzle with a slotted spoon and transfer them to the ice water bath. When all of the spätzle are cooked, place them on paper towels to dry. When dry, serve with your favorite sauce or sauté in butter.

Kartoffelkloesse

YIELD: 4 TO 6 SERVINGS • ACTIVE TIME: 30 MINUTES • TOTAL TIME: 1½ HOURS

As anyone who has visited Bavaria in Germany knows, these potato dumplings are an ideal complement to a perfectly cooked roast.

INGREDIENTS

2 lbs. Yukon Gold potatoes

½ cup all-purpose flour

1 cup potato starch, plus 2 tablespoons

3 egg yolks, lightly beaten

½ teaspoon grated nutmeg

Salt and pepper, to taste

1 Preheat the oven to 400°F. Place the potatoes on a baking sheet, prick them several times with a fork, and bake until they are soft all the way through, about 1 hour. Remove from oven, slice them open, and let cool completely.

2 When the potatoes are cool enough to handle, scoop the flesh into a mixing bowl and mash until smooth. Add the remaining ingredients and stir until well combined.

3 Grab ⅓-cup portions of the dough and roll them into balls. Place the rolled balls on a parchment-lined baking sheet. If not cooking immediately, cover with plastic wrap and refrigerate for up to 1 day. To cook the kartoffelkloesse, bring a large pot of salted water to a boil. Add the dumplings to the boiling water and cook until they are cooked through. Remove from the water, drain, and serve alongside a meat drenched in a rich gravy.

NOTE: IF YOU'RE LOOKING TO ADD A LITTLE BIT MORE TEXTURE TO THESE DUMPLINGS, FOLD 1 PEELED AND GRATED YUKON GOLD POTATO INTO THE MIXTURE BEFORE FORMING IT INTO BALLS.

Semmelknödel

YIELD: 8 SERVINGS • ACTIVE TIME: 45 MINUTES • TOTAL TIME: 3 DAYS

A great spot for leftover bread, these dumplings are right at home beside a schnitzel or sausage.

INGREDIENTS

- 1 loaf of sourdough bread, cut into ½" cubes
- 1½ sticks of unsalted butter, at room temperature
- 1 small yellow onion, chopped
- 2¼ cups whole milk
- ½ teaspoon minced fresh thyme leaves
- ½ teaspoon minced fresh rosemary leaves
- ½ teaspoon kosher salt
- ¼ teaspoon white pepper
- 6 large eggs, beaten

1 Place the bread pieces in a large mixing bowl, place the bowl in a well-ventilated spot, and let sit for 3 days.

2 Fill a Dutch oven halfway with water, bring to a simmer over medium heat, and cover. As the water warms, place 1 stick of the butter in a large skillet and melt over medium heat. Add the onion and cook until translucent, about 5 minutes. Add the milk, thyme, rosemary, salt, and white pepper and bring the mixture to a simmer. Pour the mixture over the bread pieces and let the bread soak for 10 minutes, while stirring occasionally. Add the eggs and stir to combine. Place a large piece of plastic wrap on a work surface and brush it with some of the remaining butter. Pour half of the mixture in the center of the plastic and roll into a tight log. Place another piece of plastic wrap down, brush it with more of the butter, and repeat with the remaining batter. Wrap the logs in foil, place them in the simmering water, and cook for 30 minutes. Remove, transfer to the refrigerator, and chill until they are cool, about 1 hour.

3 Place the remaining butter in a skillet and melt over medium-high heat. Cut the logs into ½" slices and place them in the melted butter. Sauté until golden brown all over, about 5 minutes on each side.

Matzo Balls

YIELD: 24 MATZO BALLS • ACTIVE TIME: 45 MINUTES • TOTAL TIME: 1½ HOURS

A recipe that strikes the perfect balance between the airy and chewy extremes that sink this delicacy.

INGREDIENTS

4 large eggs, yolks and whites separated

1 small yellow onion, grated

¼ cup chicken broth, at room temperature, plus more as needed

¼ cup rendered chicken or duck fat

1 handful of fresh parsley leaves, minced

1 teaspoon kosher salt

White pepper, to taste

1½ cups matzo meal, plus more as needed

1 Place the egg yolks, onion, broth, chicken or duck fat, parsley, salt, and pepper in a mixing bowl and stir until well combined. Add the matzo meal and stir to incorporate.

2 Place the egg whites in a separate bowl and whisk vigorously until they begin to thicken and turn glossy. Working in small increments, add the beaten whites to the matzo ball dough and fold until almost completely incorporated before adding more egg whites. If the mixture seems too runny, incorporate more matzo meal, 1 tablespoon at a time, until it is a loose paste. If the mixture seems too thick, add more broth, 1 tablespoon at a time. Cover with plastic wrap and refrigerate for 45 minutes.

3 Pinch off a piece of dough large enough to roll into a sphere the size of a golf ball. Form the dough into a ball and place on a plate. Repeat with the remaining dough and wet your hands as needed while handling the dough. If not cooking immediately, cover with plastic wrap and refrigerate for up to a day. To cook the matzo balls, add them to a boiling broth or soup one at a time. When the balls float to the surface, reduce the heat to low, cover the pot, and simmer for 20 minutes.

Dudhi Kofta

YIELD: 24 DUMPLINGS • ACTIVE TIME: 30 MINUTES • TOTAL TIME: 1½ HOURS

A great way to use up the surplus of zucchini that every summer seems to bring.

INGREDIENTS

2 lbs. zucchini, trimmed and grated

2 teaspoons kosher salt

1 small red onion, chopped

¼ cup raw cashews

2 garlic cloves, minced

1 tablespoon minced ginger

4 bird's eye chilies, seeded and minced

½ cup chickpea flour

2 tablespoons minced cilantro leaves

1 Place the grated zucchini in a bowl, add the salt, and stir to combine. Let stand for 20 minutes.

2 Place the onion, cashews, garlic, ginger, and chilies in a food processor and pulse until the mixture becomes a chunky paste.

3 Place the zucchini on a clean kitchen towel and squeeze out any excess liquid. Place the zucchini in a mixing bowl and add the onion-and-cashew paste. Stir to combine, add the chickpea flour and cilantro, and fold to combine. The dough should be slightly wet.

4 If not cooking immediately, cover the dough with plastic wrap and store in the refrigerator for up to 1 day. For instructions on forming the dough into dumplings and cooking them, follow the instructions in Step 2 on page 89.

Muthia

YIELD: 18 DUMPLINGS • ACTIVE TIME: 30 MINUTES • TOTAL TIME: 30 MINUTES

If cabbage isn't your thing, feel free to substitute any leafy green in its place.

INGREDIENTS

1 tablespoon kosher salt, plus more to taste

1 green cabbage, outer leaves reserved, remainder chopped

1½ cups chickpea flour, plus more for dusting

2 tablespoons coconut oil, melted

2 tablespoons minced ginger

2 tablespoons seeded and minced Fresno chili pepper

1 tablespoon ground coriander

1½ teaspoons ground cumin

½ teaspoon ground turmeric

1 Fill a Dutch oven with water, add the salt, and bring to a boil. Prepare an ice water bath as the water warms.

2 Add the chopped cabbage to the boiling water and cook for 1 minute. Drain and transfer the cabbage to the ice water bath. Drain and squeeze the cabbage to remove any excess liquid. Place on a kitchen towel to dry.

3 Place the chickpea flour and coconut oil in a bowl and stir to combine. Add the cabbage and the remaining ingredients and stir until the dough holds together. Place the dough on a flour-dusted work surface and knead until it is smooth and stiff. Divide the dough into 18 pieces and roll each one into a ball.

4 If not cooking immediately, place the balls on a parchment-lined baking sheet, cover with plastic wrap, and store in the refrigerator for up to 1 day. To cook the dumplings, follow the instructions in Step 1 on page 85.

Hush Puppies

YIELD: 30 HUSH PUPPIES • ACTIVE TIME: 5 MINUTES
TOTAL TIME: 1 HOUR AND 5 MINUTES

This Southern staple is usually placed alongside fried fish, but they can easily stand on their own.

INGREDIENTS

1 cup all-purpose flour

1½ cups cornmeal

2 tablespoons baking powder

2 tablespoons sugar

1 tablespoon baking soda

2 teaspoons kosher salt

½ teaspoon cayenne pepper

1¼ cups buttermilk

2 eggs

1 large yellow onion, grated

1 Place the flour, cornmeal, baking powder, sugar, baking soda, salt, and cayenne in a large bowl and stir to combine.

2 Place the buttermilk, eggs, and the grated onion and its juices in a bowl and stir to combine. Add to the dry mixture, stir to combine, and let stand for 1 hour before cooking. To cook the hush puppies, follow the instructions in Steps 1 and 2 on page 92. Serve alongside an entree or with your preferred dipping sauce.

Simple Dumplings

YIELD: 30 DUMPLINGS • ACTIVE TIME: 15 MINUTES • TOTAL TIME: 25 MINUTES

Should the sight of a simmering soup give rise to a hankering for dumplings, this simple recipe is sure to save the day.

INGREDIENTS

2 cups all-purpose flour

1 teaspoon baking powder

1 teaspoon kosher salt

1 tablespoon olive oil

2 eggs

¾ cup water

2 tablespoons minced chives

1 Place the flour, baking powder, and salt in a mixing bowl and stir until combined.

2 Add the oil, eggs, water, and chives and stir with a fork until a loose dough forms. Add tablespoons of the dough to a simmering soup and cook for 3 to 4 minutes. Cover the pot, turn off the heat, and let stand until the dumplings are cooked through, about 5 minutes.

Spiced Dumplings

YIELD: 20 DUMPLINGS • ACTIVE TIME: 15 MINUTES • TOTAL TIME: 30 MINUTES

To spice up a standard chicken-centered soup, all you need to do is add these dumplings.

INGREDIENTS

4 thick slices of crusty bread, chopped

¼ cup whole milk

2 strips of thick-cut bacon, chopped

1 shallot, minced

Leaves from 2 sprigs of thyme, minced

2 tablespoons rendered chicken or duck fat

1 egg yolk, beaten

½ teaspoon paprika

½ teaspoon cumin

½ cup all-purpose flour

Salt and pepper, to taste

1 Place the bread and the milk in a large mixing bowl and soak for 10 minutes.

2 Remove the bread and squeeze out any excess milk. Place the bread and the remaining ingredients in a bowl and stir until well combined. Taste and adjust the seasoning if necessary. Spoon out 20 piles of the mixture onto a parchment-lined baking sheet and then roll them into small balls.

3 Bring water to a boil in a small saucepan. Add the dumplings and cook for 5 minutes. Add to a soup just before it is finished cooking and cook until the dumplings are warmed through.

Steamed Buns

YIELD: 12 BUNS • ACTIVE TIME: 20 MINUTES • TOTAL TIME: 2½ HOURS

The strong glutinous web produced by high-protein bread flour is what lends these buns their irresistible chewiness.

INGREDIENTS

1 teaspoon active dry yeast

3 tablespoons water, at room temperature

1 cup bread flour, plus more for dusting

4 teaspoons sugar

2 teaspoons nonfat dry milk powder

1 teaspoon kosher salt

⅛ teaspoon baking powder

⅛ teaspoon baking soda

4 teaspoons vegetable shortening, plus more as needed

1 Place the yeast and water in the mixing bowl of a stand mixer fitted with a dough hook and let sit until the mixture becomes foamy, about 10 minutes.

2 Add the remaining ingredients and mix on low for 10 minutes. Cover the bowl with a kitchen towel and place it in a naturally warm spot until it doubles in size, about 45 minutes.

3 Place the risen dough on a flour-dusted work surface and cut into 12 pieces. Roll them into balls, cover with plastic wrap, and let them rise for 30 minutes.

4 Cut a dozen 4" squares of parchment paper. Roll each ball into a 4" oval. Grease a chopstick with shortening, gently press the chopstick down in the middle of each oval, and fold the dough over to create a bun. Place each bun on a square of parchment and let stand for 30 minutes. To cook the buns, follow the instructions in Step 4 on page 91.

Basic Dumpling Wrappers

YIELD: 32 WRAPPERS • ACTIVE TIME: 1 HOUR • TOTAL TIME: 3 HOURS

Once filled, these sturdy wrappers can be steamed, boiled, deep-fried, or pan-fried.

INGREDIENTS

2 cups all-purpose flour, plus more for dusting

¾ cup just-boiled water, plus more as needed

1 Place the flour in the mixing bowl of a stand mixer fitted with the paddle attachment. With the mixer running on low, add the water in a steady stream. Beat until the dough just holds together, adding water in 1-teaspoon increments if needed.

2 Place the dough on a flour-dusted work surface and knead until smooth and elastic, about 5 minutes. Wrap tightly in plastic and let rest at room temperature for 2 hours.

3 Cut a resealable freezer bag at the seams so that you have two squares of plastic. Place the dough on a flour-dusted work surface and cut it in half. Cover one half with plastic wrap and roll the other into a 1" thick log. Cut the log into 16 pieces. Dust each piece with flour, cover with plastic wrap, and press down gently until the rounds are ¼" thick.

4 You will want the filling prepared before starting on this step, as the dough sticks together better when it has not been exposed to the air for too long. Place the disks between the two squares of plastic and press down with a rolling pin until ⅛" thick. Transfer to a flour-dusted work surface and fill the wrappers as desired or freeze, in layers separated by parchment paper, for up to 1 month.

Wonton Wrappers

YIELD: 48 WRAPPERS • ACTIVE TIME: 1 HOUR • TOTAL TIME: 3 HOURS

Use this dough for making wontons or siu mai, which require a thin, delicate wrapper.

INGREDIENTS

- ¼ cup water, plus more as needed
- 1 large egg
- ¾ teaspoon kosher salt
- 1½ cups all-purpose flour, plus more as needed
- Cornstarch, for dusting

1 Place the water, egg, and salt in a measuring cup and whisk to combine. Place the flour in the bowl of a stand mixer fitted with the paddle attachment. With the mixer running on low speed, add the egg mixture in a steady stream and beat until the dough holds together. Add water or flour in ½-teaspoon increments if the dough is too dry or too wet, respectively. Fit the mixer with the dough hook and knead at medium speed until the dough is soft, smooth, and springs back quickly when pressed with a finger, about 10 minutes. Cover the dough tightly with plastic wrap and let rest for 2 hours.

2 Cut the dough into three even pieces. Working with one piece at a time (cover the others tightly in plastic), shape the dough into a ball. Place the dough on a flour-dusted work surface and roll it out to ½" thick. Feed the dough through a pasta maker, adjusting the setting to reduce the thickness with each pass, until the dough is thin enough that you can see your hand through it. Place the sheets on a parchment-lined baking sheet.

3 Dust a work surface with cornstarch and cut the sheets into as many 4" squares (for wontons) or 3" rounds (for siu mai) as possible. Pile the cut wrappers on top of each other and fill as desired, or cover in plastic wrap and refrigerate for up to 3 days.

Crystal Dumpling Wrappers

YIELD: 18 WRAPPERS • ACTIVE TIME: 45 MINUTES • TOTAL TIME: 45 MINUTES

Make sure you have your filling ready to go, as these wrappers do not keep for long once made.

INGREDIENTS

1 cup wheat starch, plus more for dusting

½ cup cornstarch

1¼ cups boiling water

1 tablespoon grapeseed or safflower oil

1 Cut a resealable freezer bag at the seams so that you have two squares of plastic and set aside. Place the wheat starch and cornstarch in a heatproof medium bowl. Add the boiling water and oil. Using a rubber spatula, stir the ingredients until a loose dough forms. Turn the dough out onto a work surface dusted with wheat starch and knead until it is smooth and slowly bounces back into place when pressed with a finger. This should take about 10 minutes.

2 Roll the dough into a 1½" thick log. Cut it into 18 equal pieces, dust them with wheat starch, and cover with plastic wrap. Press down lightly on the pieces to create a disk that is roughly ¼" thick. Place the disks between the two squares of plastic and press down with a rolling pin until ⅛" thick. Dredge any disks that feel sticky with wheat starch, place on a parchment-lined baking sheet, and fill as desired.

Baozi Wrappers

YIELD: 16 WRAPPERS • ACTIVE TIME: 45 MINUTES • TOTAL TIME: 1½ HOURS

Baozi reside in the delectable space between steamed buns and potstickers.

INGREDIENTS

- 1 tablespoon instant yeast
- 1½ cups water, at room temperature
- ¼ cup vegetable oil, plus more as needed
- ¼ cup sugar, plus 1 teaspoon
- ½ teaspoon kosher salt
- 4 teaspoons baking powder
- 2 cups all-purpose flour, plus more for dusting
- 2 cups bread flour

1 Place the yeast, water, and oil in a small bowl and let stand until foamy, about 10 minutes.

2 Place the sugar, salt, baking powder, and flours in a food processor and pulse for 15 seconds to combine. With the food processor running on low speed, add the yeast mixture and keep it running until it comes together as a slightly tacky dough. Place the dough on a flour-dusted work surface and knead until it is smooth, about 3 minutes. Place the dough in a bowl greased with vegetable oil, cover with a kitchen towel, and let rise in a naturally warm place until it has doubled in size, about 30 minutes.

3 Place the dough on the flour-dusted work surface, cut it in half, and roll each half into a log. Cut each log into eight pieces. Roll each piece into a 4" circle and fill as desired. Cover the unrolled pieces of dough with a kitchen towel so that they do not dry out. To cook the filled baozi, follow the instructions in Step 3 on page 111.

Samosa Wrappers

YIELD: 16 WRAPPERS • ACTIVE TIME: 20 MINUTES • TOTAL TIME: 20 MINUTES

Maida flour is finely milled to remove all of the bran from the wheat, producing a soft result that closely resembles cake flour.

INGREDIENTS

2 cups maida flour, plus more for dusting

¼ teaspoon kosher salt

2 tablespoons vegetable oil

½ cup water, plus more as needed

1 Place the flour and salt in a mixing bowl and use your hands to combine. Add the oil and work the mixture with your hands until it is a coarse meal.

2 Add the water and knead the mixture until a smooth, firm dough forms. If the dough is too dry, incorporate more water, 1 tablespoon at a time.

3 Divide the dough into eight pieces and roll each one out into a 6" circle on a flour-dusted work surface. Cut the circles in half and brush the flat edge of each with water. Fold one corner of the flat edge toward the other to make a cone and pinch to seal. Fill each cone one-third of the way with your chosen filling, brush the opening with water, and pinch to seal. Place the sealed samosas on a parchment-lined baking sheet. To cook the filled samosas, follow the instructions in Step 4 on page 157.

Kroppkakor Wrappers

YIELD: 16 WRAPPERS • ACTIVE TIME: 25 MINUTES • TOTAL TIME: 50 MINUTES

If the lingonberries that traditionally accompany these Swedish dumplings prove tough to find, serve with a black currant jelly.

INGREDIENTS

1¾ lbs. Yukon Gold potatoes, peeled and chopped

1½ teaspoons kosher salt

2 large eggs, lightly beaten

1½ cups potato flour

½ cup all-purpose flour, plus more as needed

1 Place the potatoes in a saucepan, cover with water, and bring to a boil. Cook until fork-tender, about 15 minutes. Drain, transfer to a mixing bowl, and let cool for 10 minutes. Mash until smooth, add the remaining ingredients, and beat until the mixture forms a dough that is smooth and not sticky. If the dough is too sticky, incorporate more all-purpose flour, adding 1 teaspoon at a time.

2 Pinch off a piece of dough large enough to roll into a sphere the size of a golf ball. Place it on a flour-dusted work surface and roll into a ball. Flatten the balls into disks and fill as desired. To cook the filled kroppkakor, follow the instructions in Step 3 on page 140.

Pierogi Wrappers

YIELD: 36 WRAPPERS • ACTIVE TIME: 1 HOUR • TOTAL TIME: 2 HOURS

Endlessly versatile and infinitely comforting, feel free to stuff these dumplings with whatever pops into your mind.

INGREDIENTS

3 cups all-purpose flour, plus more as needed

½ teaspoon kosher salt, plus more to taste

4 tablespoons unsalted butter

⅔ cup sour cream, at room temperature

1 large egg, beaten

Water, as needed

1 Place the flour, salt, butter, and sour cream in the mixing bowl of a stand mixer fitted with the paddle attachment. Beat on medium speed until a crumbly dough forms, about 5 minutes.

2 Place the egg in a measuring cup and add enough water for the mixture to measure ¾ cup. Beat until combined and pour into the mixing bowl. Beat on medium speed until the dough holds together and is no longer sticky. If the dough is sticky, incorporate more flour, 1 teaspoon at a time. Cover with plastic wrap and let rest at room temperature for 1 hour.

3 Place the dough on a flour-dusted work surface and roll out to ¼" thick. Use a mason jar or biscuit cutter to cut as many 3" rounds from the dough as possible. Place the rounds on a parchment-lined baking sheet and lightly dust with flour. When you have as many as you can fit in a single layer, cover with another piece of parchment. Fill as desired. To cook the filled pierogi, follow the instructions in Step 4 on page 137.

Perfect Pairings

Now that you've started to make your way into the world of dumplings, it's time to master the elements that make them a treasured component of cuisines around the world. Luckily, the preparations featured in the previous chapter don't require much ornamentation. Often, a simple sauce, such as the sage butter featured on page 70 or the remoulade sauce that the people of Louisiana made their own after the French left it behind, will do the trick.

Yes, dumplings are a blank canvas that rewards the creative, but when you need something that is guaranteed to hit the spot, these recipes are certain to deliver.

Gnocchi in Brown Butter

YIELD: 4 TO 6 SERVINGS • ACTIVE TIME: 30 MINUTES • TOTAL TIME: 45 MINUTES

The addition of *beurre noisette* (brown butter) gives this traditional dumpling an earthy and nutty flavor.

INGREDIENTS

4 sticks of unsalted butter

Salt, to taste

Potato Gnocchi (see page 11)

1 Place the butter in a Dutch oven and cook over the lowest possible heat until it is golden brown and gives off a nutty aroma, 5 to 10 minutes. Remove from heat and set aside.

2 Bring a large pot of salted water to a boil. Working in batches of 20 gnocchi, add them to the boiling water and stir so that they do not stick to the bottom. When they float to the top, cook for another minute, remove with a strainer, and shake to remove excess moisture. Place them in the brown butter.

3 Sauté the gnocchi in the brown butter until crispy on each side. Drizzle some of the brown butter over the top and serve immediately.

Gnocchi with Truffled Cheese Sauce

YIELD: 6 SERVINGS • ACTIVE TIME: 20 MINUTES • TOTAL TIME: 35 MINUTES

Chewy gnocchi in a creamy cheese sauce is the ultimate testament to the value of simplicity in the kitchen.

INGREDIENTS

2 cups heavy cream

1½ cups grated Parmesan cheese

4 oz. Fontina cheese, grated

1½ teaspoons truffle oil

Salt and white pepper, to taste

Potato Gnocchi (see page 11)

Basil, chopped, for garnish

1 Place the cream in a saucepan and warm over low heat until it is almost bubbling. Add the cheeses, truffle oil, and white pepper and cook, while stirring occasionally, until the cheeses have melted. Place a few tablespoons of the sauce in a warmed bowl that is large enough to hold all of the gnocchi.

2 Bring a large pot of salted water to a boil. Working in batches of 20 gnocchi, add them to the boiling water and stir so that they do not stick to the bottom. When they float to the top, cook for another minute, remove with a strainer, and shake to remove excess moisture. Place in the bowl containing the sauce and toss to coat. Repeat until all of the gnocchi are cooked and coated, replenishing the sauce in the bowl as needed. Garnish with the basil and serve immediately.

Sweet Potato Gnocchi with Sage Butter

YIELD: 6 SERVINGS • ACTIVE TIME: 20 MINUTES • TOTAL TIME: 35 MINUTES

Whoever had the idea to add sage to brown butter was a wise individual indeed.

INGREDIENTS

Salt, to taste

2 tablespoons olive oil

Sweet Potato Gnocchi (see page 12)

1 stick of unsalted butter

1 tablespoon chopped sage leaves

2 cups arugula

½ cup toasted walnuts, chopped

1 Bring a large pot of salted water to a boil and place the olive oil in a large bowl. Working in batches of 20, add the gnocchi to the boiling water and stir to keep them from sticking to the bottom. The gnocchi will eventually float to the surface. Cook for 1 more minute, remove, and transfer to the bowl containing the olive oil. Toss to coat and place on a parchment-lined baking sheet to cool.

2 Place the butter in a sauté pan and cook over medium heat until it begins to brown. Add the sage and cook until the bubbles start to dissipate. Place the arugula in a bowl and set it aside.

3 Working in batches, add the gnocchi to the sauté pan, toss to evenly coat, and cook until they have a nice sear on one side. Transfer to the bowl of arugula and toss to combine. Plate and top with the toasted walnuts.

Gnocchi in Mushroom Sauce

YIELD: 6 SERVINGS • ACTIVE TIME: 45 MINUTES • TOTAL TIME: 45 MINUTES

The key to this sauce is the key to preparing mushrooms in general: cook off their liquid to concentrate their flavor.

INGREDIENTS

- Salt and white pepper, to taste
- 2 tablespoons unsalted butter
- ¼ cup white truffle oil
- 2 garlic cloves, crushed
- 1 lb. cremini mushrooms, stemmed, rinsed, and sliced
- 1 teaspoon grated nutmeg
- ½ cup heavy cream
- Arugula & Boursin Gnocchi (see page 15)

1 Bring a large pot of salted water to a boil. Place the butter and half of the truffle oil in a large skillet and warm over medium heat. When the butter has melted and stopped foaming, add the garlic and cook, while stirring occasionally, until it begins to turn golden, about 3 minutes. Discard the garlic and add the mushrooms. Season with salt and pepper and cook, while stirring occasionally, until the mushrooms' liquid has evaporated, about 14 minutes. Add the nutmeg and cream, stir to combine, and cook until heated through. Cover and set aside.

2 Working in batches of 20, add the gnocchi to the boiling water and stir to keep them from sticking to the bottom. The gnocchi will eventually float to the surface. Cook for 1 more minute, remove, and transfer to a bowl. Tent with foil to keep warm while you cook the remaining gnocchi.

3 Place the gnocchi on warmed plates. Season the sauce to taste and ladle it over the gnocchi. Drizzle the remaining truffle oil over the top and serve immediately.

Baccalà Gnocchi in Radicchio Sauce

YIELD: 8 SERVINGS • ACTIVE TIME: 30 MINUTES • TOTAL TIME: 45 MINUTES

If you'd prefer a more subdued radicchio, consider using the Treviso variety, which looks like a crimson endive.

INGREDIENTS

3 tablespoons unsalted butter

1 large head of radicchio, cored and shredded

Salt and white pepper, to taste

3 tablespoons warm water (105°F)

1½ cups heavy cream

Baccalà Gnocchi (see page 16)

Juice of ½ lemon

½ cup fresh parsley leaves, chopped

1 Place the butter in a large skillet and warm over medium heat. When the butter has melted and stopped foaming, add the radicchio, season with salt and white pepper, and cook, while stirring occasionally, until the radicchio wilts, about 5 minutes. Add the warm water and cook until the radicchio is tender, about 4 minutes. Using a slotted spoon, transfer the radicchio to a bowl and cover to keep warm. Place the cream in the skillet and bring to a gentle boil. Reduce the heat to low and simmer until the sauce has thickened and reduced, about 15 minutes.

2 While the sauce is simmering, bring a large pot of salted water to a boil. Adjust the heat so that the water is boiling gently and not furiously. Working in batches of 20, add the gnocchi to the boiling water and do not stir. The gnocchi will eventually float to the surface. Cook for 1 more minute, remove, and transfer to the skillet containing the cream sauce. When all of the gnocchi have been added, stir in the lemon juice, parsley, and raddichio and cook, while stirring, until everything is warmed through. Serve immediately.

Chocolate & Cheese Gnocchi in Walnut Sauce

YIELD: 4 SERVINGS • ACTIVE TIME: 20 MINUTES • TOTAL TIME: 50 MINUTES

This decadent sauce hails from the herb-laden hills of Liguria in northwestern Italy.

INGREDIENTS

1 cup day-old bread pieces

1 cup walnuts

1 garlic clove, sliced thin

¼ cup bread crumbs

Leaves from 2 sprigs of marjoram, chopped

3 tablespoons walnut oil

3 tablespoons heavy cream

5 tablespoons unsalted butter, at room temperature

Salt, to taste

Chocolate & Cheese Gnocchi (see page 19)

½ cup spinach

1 Place the bread pieces in a small bowl, cover with warm water, and let soak for 30 minutes. Drain and then squeeze the bread to remove as much water as possible. Place the soaked bread cubes, walnuts, garlic, bread crumbs, and half of the marjoram in a food processor and blitz until you have a smooth paste. Transfer the paste to a mixing bowl, add the walnut oil, cream, and 3 tablespoons of the butter, and season generously with salt. Whisk to combine and set the mixture aside.

2 Bring a large pot of salted water to a boil. Working in batches of 20, add the gnocchi to the boiling water and stir to keep them from sticking to the bottom. The gnocchi will eventually float to the surface. Cook for 1 more minute, remove, and place in the mixing bowl with the sauce.

3 Place the remaining butter in a large skillet and melt over medium heat. Add the spinach, cook until wilted, and then add the gnocchi and the sauce. Cook, while stirring, until everything is warmed through. Garnish with the remaining marjoram and serve immediately.

Chickpea Gnocchi in Spicy Pork Sauce

YIELD: 6 TO 8 SERVINGS • ACTIVE TIME: 30 MINUTES • TOTAL TIME: 2 HOURS

This aromatic meat sauce will adhere to the gnocchi's ridges and clue you in to just why they are so important.

INGREDIENTS

6 tablespoons unsalted butter

1 yellow onion, grated

2 celery stalks, grated

Salt, to taste

1½ lbs. ground pork

1 cup milk

5 whole cloves

1 cup chicken broth

2 tablespoons tomato paste

2 bay leaves

Red pepper flakes, to taste

Chickpea Gnocchi (see page 20)

1 Place the butter in a Dutch oven and melt over medium-high heat. Add the onion and celery, season with salt, and stir to combine. When the vegetables start to sizzle, reduce the heat to low, cover, and cook, while stirring occasionally, until the vegetables are very tender, about 30 minutes.

2 Add the ground pork, raise the heat to medium-high, and cook, while using a wooden spoon to break up the meat, until the pork starts to brown. Add the milk and cook until it has evaporated, about 10 minutes. Add the cloves, cook for 2 minutes, and then add the broth, tomato paste, bay leaves, and red pepper flakes. Bring to a boil, reduce the heat to low, cover, and simmer for 45 minutes, while stirring occasionally. You'll know the sauce is done when the fat has separated and is bubbling on the surface.

3 While the sauce is simmering, bring a large pot of salted water to a boil. Working in batches of 20, add the gnocchi to the boiling water and stir to keep them from sticking to the bottom. The gnocchi will eventually float to the surface. Cook for 1 more minute and then transfer them to a bowl. Tent with foil to keep warm. When all of the gnocchi have been cooked and the sauce is done, divide the gnocchi between the serving plates and ladle the sauce over them.

Canederli with Speck & Caraway Crumbs

YIELD: 4 TO 6 SERVINGS • ACTIVE TIME: 10 MINUTES • TOTAL TIME: 30 MINUTES

If speck proves difficult to track down, prosciutto can easily be substituted.

INGREDIENTS

1½ tablespoons olive oil

¾ cup bread crumbs

1½ teaspoons caraway seeds

Salt and pepper, to taste

Canederli (see page 23)

4 tablespoons unsalted butter

¼ lb. speck, minced

½ cup thinly sliced chives

1 Warm a large skillet over medium heat for 2 minutes. Add the olive oil and raise the heat to medium-high. When the oil starts to shimmer, add the bread crumbs and caraway seeds, season with salt and pepper, and cook until the bread crumbs are a deep golden brown, about 3 minutes. Transfer to a bowl and set aside.

2 Bring a large pot of salted water to a boil. Add all of the Canederli, reduce the heat to medium, and cook until just cooked through, about 15 minutes. Transfer the cooked Canederli to a warm platter and set aside.

3 Place the butter in a large skillet and warm over medium-high heat. When it's melted and stops foaming, add the Canederli and cook, carefully turning them over every minute or so, until they are golden brown, about 4 minutes. Add the speck and chives and cook, while stirring, until warmed through. Divide the mixture between warmed serving plates and top with the caraway bread crumbs.

Pizzicotti with Lamb Ragù

YIELD: 6 SERVINGS • ACTIVE TIME: 1 HOUR • TOTAL TIME: 3½ HOURS

A small, rustic dumpling from Tuscany, *pizzicotti* translates to "pinches," most likely because they are formed by pinching off pieces of yeasted dough.

INGREDIENTS

For the Pizzicotti

4 cups all-purpose flour

2½ teaspoons active dry yeast

2 teaspoons kosher salt, plus more to taste

1¼ cups warm water (105°F)

Semolina flour, for dusting

For the Lamb Ragù

2 tablespoons extra virgin olive oil

2 small onions, minced

2 celery stalks, minced

Salt and pepper, to taste

2 lbs. ground lamb

1 cup dry red wine

3 to 4 small sprigs of thyme, leaves removed and minced

2 small sprigs of fresh marjoram, minced

1 small dried chili pepper

2 (28 oz.) cans of peeled whole San Marzano tomatoes, crushed by hand

For Garnish

Parmesan cheese, grated

1 To prepare the pizzicotti, whisk the all-purpose flour, yeast, and salt together in a large bowl, add the water gradually, and work the mixture with a fork until it starts holding together. Work the dough with your hands until it feels firm and dry. Transfer the dough to a work surface dusted with semolina flour and knead the dough until it is very smooth and gently pulls back into place when stretched, 8 to 10 minutes. Place the dough in a large bowl, cover with plastic wrap, and let rise in a naturally warm place until it doubles in size, about 1 hour.

2 While the pizzicotti is on its initial rise, prepare the lamb ragù. Place the olive oil in a Dutch oven and warm over medium-high heat. Add the onions, celery, and a couple of pinches of salt and stir to combine. When the mixture starts to sizzle, reduce the heat to low, cover, and cook, while stirring occasionally, until the vegetables are very soft and slightly dark, about 30 minutes.

3 Add the ground lamb to the pot and cook, while breaking it apart with a wooden spoon, until it is no longer pink. Raise the heat to medium-high, add the wine, and cook for 5 minutes. Add the thyme, marjoram, and chili pepper, stir, and cook for 2 minutes. Add the tomatoes and their juices, season with salt and pepper, stir, and bring to a boil. Reduce the heat to medium-low and simmer, while stirring occasionally, until the sauce has visibly thickened and the fat has separated and is bubbling on the surface, about 2 hours.

4 Remove the pizzicotti dough from the bowl and, holding it in your hands, knead it just enough to remove any air trapped inside. Place it on a parchment-lined baking sheet, cover with a kitchen towel, and let rise for another hour in a warm place.

5 Bring a large pot of salted water to a boil. Knead the dough to remove any air, pinch off peanut-sized pieces of the dough, and drop them in the boiling water, working in batches if necessary. Cook until they float to the surface, 2 to 3 minutes. Drain, transfer to a bowl, add the ragù, and toss to combine. Garnish each serving with grated Parmesan.

Spinach Malfatti

YIELD: 4 SERVINGS • ACTIVE TIME: 40 MINUTES • TOTAL TIME: 50 MINUTES

Malfatti means "badly formed" in Italian. Fortunately, looks are often deceiving.

INGREDIENTS

For the Tomato Sauce

4 lbs. ripe plum tomatoes, concasse (see page 91)

2 tablespoons olive oil

1 yellow onion, grated

Salt, to taste

Handful of basil leaves

For the Spinach Malfatti

2 lbs. fresh spinach, stems removed

4 large eggs, lightly beaten

1¼ cups all-purpose flour

1 teaspoon grated nutmeg

Salt and white pepper, to taste

1 To prepare the tomato sauce, place the tomatoes in a food processor or blender and puree until smooth. Place the olive oil in a Dutch oven and warm over medium heat. Add the onion and a pinch of salt and cook, while stirring frequently, until the onion has softened, about 10 minutes. Add the tomatoes and two pinches of salt and stir. Bring to a boil, reduce the heat to low, cover, and simmer until thickened, about 20 minutes.

2 While the sauce is simmering, prepare the malfatti. Warm a large skillet over medium-high heat. Add the spinach, cook until the leaves have wilted but are still bright green, and then transfer to a colander. When cool enough to handle, squeeze the spinach to remove any remaining water. Mince the spinach and place it in a mixing bowl with the eggs. Stir to combine, add the flour, nutmeg, and a few pinches of salt and white pepper, and stir until the mixture looks like thick muffin batter.

3 Bring a large pot of salted water to a boil. Working in batches of 15, add teaspoons of the mixture to the water and cook until they float to the surface, 2 to 3 minutes. Remove with a strainer, transfer to a large warmed bowl, and tent it with foil. When all of the malfatti have been cooked, add the basil to the sauce and cover the Dutch oven. After 5 minutes, add the sauce to the bowl of malfatti, toss to combine, and serve immediately.

Muthia with Cilantro Yogurt

YIELD: 6 SERVINGS • ACTIVE TIME: 20 MINUTES • TOTAL TIME: 30 MINUTES

A serving board freighted with sliced veggies is another great spot for this deliciously fresh yogurt.

INGREDIENTS

Muthia (see page 40)

1 cup cilantro leaves

1 cup baby spinach

¼ cup cold water

2 cups plain yogurt

Pinch of cayenne pepper

1 Place 1" of water in a large pot and place a steaming tray over the pot. Line the steaming tray with the cabbage leaves reserved from preparing the Muthia and place the dumplings on top. Bring the water to a boil and steam the dumplings until they are shiny and firm, about 20 minutes.

2 While the dumplings are steaming, bring water to a boil in another saucepan and prepare an ice water bath. Add the cilantro and spinach to the boiling water, cook for 1 minute, drain, and transfer the cilantro and spinach to the ice water bath. Drain, press down to squeeze as much water out of the mixture as you can, and transfer the mixture to a food processor.

3 Add the water and half of the yogurt to the food processor and puree until smooth. Place this mixture, the cayenne pepper, and the remaining yogurt in a bowl, stir to combine, and serve alongside the steamed dumplings.

Takoyaki

YIELD: 4 SERVINGS • ACTIVE TIME: 20 MINUTES • TOTAL TIME: 20 MINUTES

The perfect party food: unusual and delicious enough to impress and simple enough to partner with a nice, cold beer.

INGREDIENTS

2 teaspoons sake

2 teaspoons mirin

2 teaspoons soy sauce

2 teaspoons oyster sauce

2 teaspoons Worcestershire sauce

1 tablespoon sugar

1 tablespoon ketchup

Salt and white pepper, to taste

2 tablespoons water, plus more as needed

1 large egg

1½ cups Chicken Stock (see page 182)

¾ cup all-purpose flour

1 cup minced cooked octopus

2 scallion greens, sliced thin

¼ cup minced pickled ginger

Takoyaki Sauce (see sidebar), for serving

1 Place the sake, mirin, soy sauce, oyster sauce, Worcestershire sauce, sugar, ketchup, salt, and white pepper in a mixing bowl and stir to combine. Set the mixture aside.

2 Place the water, the egg, and stock in a bowl and stir until combined. Sprinkle the flour over the mixture and stir until all of the flour has been incorporated and the mixture is a thick batter. Add the sake-and-mirin mixture and stir to incorporate. Pour the batter into a measuring cup with a spout.

3 Coat the wells of an aebleskiver pan or a muffin pan with nonstick cooking spray and place it over medium heat. When the pan is hot, fill the wells of the pan halfway and add a pinch of octopus, scallion, and pickled ginger to each. Fill the wells the rest of the way with the batter, until they are almost overflowing. Cook the dumplings for approximately 2 minutes and use a chopstick to flip each one over. Turn the fritters as needed until they are golden brown on both sides and piping hot. Serve immediately alongside the Takoyaki Sauce.

Takoyaki Sauce

INGREDIENTS

½ cup Worcestershire sauce
1 tablespoon mentsuyu or chicken broth
2¼ teaspoons sugar
1½ teaspoons ketchup

Place all of the ingredients in a small bowl and whisk to combine. Season to taste and serve.

Dudhi Kofta Curry

YIELD: 4 TO 6 SERVINGS • ACTIVE TIME: 30 MINUTES • TOTAL TIME: 30 MINUTES

An unorthodox tomato sauce featuring cashews and raisins is certain to open more than a few eyes.

INGREDIENTS

- 4 cups vegetable oil, plus 2 tablespoons
- 1 teaspoon cumin seeds
- 1 red onion, chopped
- 4 bird's eye chilies, seeded and minced
- 2 tablespoons raw cashews
- 2 tablespoons golden raisins
- 1 (28 oz.) can of diced tomatoes
- 1 teaspoon kosher salt
- Dough from Dudhi Kofta (see page 39)
- ¼ cup milk
- ¼ cup heavy cream
- ¼ teaspoon ground turmeric
- 2 pinches of black pepper
- 2 pinches of cinnamon
- 2 pinches of ground cloves
- 2 pinches of nutmeg
- 2 pinches of ground cardamom

1 Place the 2 tablespoons of vegetable oil in a saucepan and warm over medium-high heat. Add the cumin seeds, cook until fragrant, and then add the onion, chilies, cashews, and raisins and cook until the onion and cashews are slightly browned, about 5 minutes. Add the tomatoes and salt, cook for another 2 minutes, transfer the sauce to a food processor, and puree until smooth.

2 Place the remaining oil in a Dutch oven and heat it to 300°F over medium-high heat. As the oil warms, form tablespoons of the dough into balls and place them on a parchment-lined baking sheet. When the oil is ready, place the dumplings in the oil and fry until golden brown, about 5 minutes. Work in batches if necessary. Transfer the cooked dumplings to a paper towel-lined plate to drain.

3 Place the sauce back in the pan, add the remaining ingredients, and stir to combine. Heat until warmed through, ladle into warmed bowls, and top with the dumplings.

Steamed Pork Buns

YIELD: 6 SERVINGS • ACTIVE TIME: 1 HOUR • TOTAL TIME: 24 HOURS

As you'll see once you prepare them, these started popping up on menus everywhere for a good reason.

INGREDIENTS

Steamed Buns (see page 46)

For the Pork Belly

6 cups water

1 teaspoon fennel seeds

2 star anise pods

1 cinnamon stick

1 teaspoon peppercorns

6 whole cloves

1 bay leaf

¼ cup kosher salt

1½ lbs. pork belly, fat-side scored ¼" deep

For the Pickled Tomatoes

¼ cup white wine vinegar

1½ tablespoons brown sugar

2 teaspoons kosher salt

½ teaspoon minced garlic

2 teaspoons mustard seeds

¼ teaspoon cracked peppercorns

1 teaspoon ground cumin

¼ teaspoon cayenne pepper

¼ teaspoon turmeric

1½ tablespoons olive oil

1 plum tomato, concasse (see sidebar)

1 Start the preparations the night before making the Steamed Buns. To prepare the pork belly, place the water, fennel seeds, star anise pods, cinnamon stick, peppercorns, whole cloves, bay leaf, and salt in a saucepan and bring to a boil. Turn off the heat and let the mixture cool completely. Place the pork belly in a roasting pan and pour the cooled liquid into the pan. Place the pan in the refrigerator overnight.

2 To prepare the pickled tomatoes, place all of the ingredients, except for the tomato, in a saucepan and bring to a simmer over medium heat. Remove from heat, let cool completely, and then add the tomato. Cover and chill in the refrigerator overnight.

3 Preheat oven to 450°F and rinse the pork belly. Place the pork belly on a rimmed baking sheet, scored-side up, place it in the oven, and roast for 30 minutes. Lower the temperature to 275°F and roast until it is tender, but not mushy, about 1 hour. While the pork belly is roasting, prepare the Steamed Buns.

4 When the pork belly is done, remove and let sit for 20 minutes. Place 1" of water in a saucepan and bring to a boil. Place a steaming tray over the pan and, working in batches if necessary, place the buns in the steaming tray, making sure to leave them on the parchment. Steam for 10 minutes. Slice the pork belly thin and fill the buns with it. Top with the pickled tomatoes and serve.

Tomato Concasse

Concasse, French for "to crush or grind," refers to tomatoes that have been peeled, seeded, and then chopped. To do this easily, boil enough water for a tomato to be submerged and add a pinch of salt. Prepare an ice water bath and score the top of the tomato with a paring knife, being sure to only cut the skin. Place the tomato in the boiling water for 30 seconds, carefully remove it, and place it in the ice bath. Once the tomato is cool, remove from the water and peel with the paring knife. Cut into quarters, remove the seeds, and chop.

Hush Puppies with Remoulade Sauce

YIELD: 6 SERVINGS • ACTIVE TIME: 20 MINUTES • TOTAL TIME: 20 MINUTES

This French sauce has come into its own thanks to the culinary genius native to Louisiana.

INGREDIENTS

Vegetable oil, for frying

Hush Puppies (see page 43)

1 cup mayonnaise

2 tablespoons whole grain mustard

1 teaspoon Cajun seasoning

1 tablespoon sweet paprika

1 tablespoon pickle juice or fresh lemon juice

1 tablespoon hot sauce, or to taste

1½ teaspoons minced garlic

2 tablespoons minced fresh parsley (optional)

Salt and pepper, to taste

1 Add vegetable oil to a large Dutch oven until it is 2" deep. Warm over medium-high heat until it is 350°F.

2 Drop tablespoons of the batter into the oil, while making sure to not crowd the Dutch oven. Cook, while flipping the Hush Puppies over halfway through, until they are crispy and golden brown, about 3 to 4 minutes. Transfer the cooked Hush Puppies to a paper towel-lined plate to drain.

3 To prepare the remoulade sauce, place all of the remaining ingredients in a bowl and stir to combine. Serve alongside the fried Hush Puppies.

Meat-Filled Treats

When most people think of dumplings, the delectable parcels contained in this chapter are what the mind flashes upon. And with good reason. When that chewy wrapper gives way to a warm and savory filling centered around meat, the combination of tastes and textures produce unforgettable culinary experiences.

With all the classics—gyoza, siu mai, potstickers, and empanadas—on hand, plus innovations like a chicken liver-stuffed matzo ball and a tender dough filled with bulgogi, the darling of the Korean BBQ world, this chapter will take you on a trip that you'll never forget.

Beef Bulgogi Dumplings

YIELD: 4 TO 6 SERVINGS • ACTIVE TIME: 1 HOUR • TOTAL TIME: 13 HOURS

Stuffing a traditional Korean BBQ recipe into a dumpling is a tremendous idea, especially when it's paired with a spicy aioli.

INGREDIENTS

1 garlic clove, minced

1 tablespoon soy sauce

2 teaspoons gochugaru (Korean hot pepper flakes) or ½ teaspoon red pepper flakes

2 teaspoons minced ginger

2 teaspoons light brown sugar

2 teaspoons sesame oil

½ lb. sirloin steak, trimmed and sliced into thin strips

6 tablespoons vegetable oil

Salt and pepper, to taste

2 eggs, beaten

24 Basic Dumpling Wrappers (see page 49)

Charred Scallion Aioli (see sidebar)

Scallion greens, diced, for garnish

Peanuts, crushed, for garnish

1 Place the garlic, soy sauce, gochugaru or red pepper flakes, ginger, brown sugar, sesame oil, and steak in a small bowl or resealable plastic bag. Gently shake to combine, place in the refrigerator, and let marinate for 12 hours. Remove approximately 30 minutes before preparing the dumplings and allow to come to room temperature.

2 Warm a sauté pan over medium-high heat until it starts to smoke. Add 1 tablespoon of the vegetable oil and the marinated steak and cook for 1 minute. Turn the meat over and cook for an additional 2 minutes. Remove from the pan and let cool on a baking sheet. When cool enough to handle, chop the meat into small pieces.

3 Dip a finger into the beaten eggs and run it along the edge of a wrapper. Place a tablespoon of meat in the center, fold the circle into a half-moon, and seal tightly.

Repeat until all of the dumplings are filled and sealed. Fill a saucepan with 1" of water and bring to a boil. Place a steaming tray over the water, add the dumplings, and steam for 6 minutes. Take care not to crowd the steaming tray, and work in batches if necessary. Remove the dumplings and let cool.

4 Place the remaining vegetable oil in a sauté pan or wok and heat over medium heat. When the oil starts to shimmer, add the dumplings in batches and cook until golden brown, about 1 minute on each side. Garnish with the scallion greens and peanuts and serve with the Charred Scallion Aioli.

Charred Scallion Aioli

INGREDIENTS

- ¾ cup vegetable oil, plus 1 tablespoon
- 6 scallion whites
- 2 garlic cloves
- ¼ cup peanuts
- 1 tablespoon hot water (125°F)
- 1 teaspoon Dijon mustard
- 1 tablespoon gochugaru or red pepper flakes
- Juice of ½ lemon
- 1 tablespoon soy sauce
- 2 eggs
- ¼ cup sesame oil

1 Place the tablespoon of vegetable oil in a large sauté pan and warm over medium-high heat. When the oil starts to shimmer, add the scallions and cook until golden brown all over, about 5 minutes. Reduce heat to medium, add the garlic, peanuts, and hot water and cook until the garlic and peanuts are golden brown, about 5 minutes. Turn off heat and let cool.

2 Transfer the contents of the pan to a food processor and puree until smooth. Add the mustard, gochugaru or red pepper flakes, lemon juice, soy sauce, and eggs and blitz until incorporated. Reduce the speed to low and add the sesame oil and remaining vegetable oil in slow streams. When all of the oils have been incorporated, transfer the aioli to the refrigerator and chill for 1 hour before using.

Crispy Char Siu Pork Wontons

YIELD: 6 TO 8 SERVINGS • ACTIVE TIME: 45 MINUTES • TOTAL TIME: 10 HOURS

This sweet-and-savory cornerstone of Cantonese BBQ shops has countless uses, as you will see once you get the hang of it.

INGREDIENTS

3 garlic cloves, minced

3 tablespoons sugar

¾ teaspoon Chinese five-spice powder

¼ cup hoisin sauce

3 tablespoons honey

2 tablespoons rice wine vinegar

¼ cup soy sauce

1 tablespoon sesame oil

2 lbs. boneless pork shoulder, cut into 1½" thick strips

4 cups vegetable oil

1 egg, beaten

1 tablespoon water

24 square Wonton Wrappers (see page 50)

1 Place the garlic, sugar, five-spice, hoisin sauce, honey, vinegar, soy sauce, and sesame oil in a bowl and stir to combine. Remove one-third of the mixture and place it in the refrigerator. Add the strips of pork to the remaining marinade, stir to coat, cover, and place in the refrigerator for at least 8 hours, and overnight if time allows. Stir the pork three or four times as it marinates. Remove the pork and reserved marinade approximately 45 minutes before you start cooking and allow it to come to room temperature.

2 Preheat the oven to 475°F, line a baking sheet with aluminum foil, and place a roasting rack on top. Place the pork on the rack, leaving about 1" between each piece, and roast in the oven for approximately 30 minutes, while basting the pork every 10 minutes. To baste, place some of the reserved marinade in a small bowl, submerge individual pieces of the pork in it, and then return the pork to the oven.

Cook until the interior of the pork reads 145°F on an instant read thermometer. Remove from the oven and let cool. While the pork is cooling, add the reserved marinade that did not come in contact with any pork to a small pot and cook over medium-high heat until it has reduced to a thick sauce. When the pork is cool enough to handle, shred the pork, add it to the reduction, and stir to coat.

3 Place the vegetable oil in a Dutch oven and heat to 350°F over medium-high heat. As the oil warms, beat the egg and water together. Place 1 tablespoon of the pork mixture in the center of a wrapper, dip a finger into the egg wash, and rub the edge of the wrapper. Bring the corners together, pinch to seal, and repeat with the remaining wrappers.

4 Working in batches, place the wontons in the oil and fry until golden brown, about 3 minutes. Drain on paper towels and let cool briefly before serving.

Gun Mandu

YIELD: 4 SERVINGS • ACTIVE TIME: 1 HOUR • TOTAL TIME: 1½ HOURS

These popular Korean dumplings are typically poached in a broth, but they are also great pan-fried or steamed.

INGREDIENTS

½ lb. extra-firm tofu

1 cup bean sprouts, blanched and chopped

2 scallions, sliced, greens reserved for dipping sauce

1 yellow onion, chopped

2 garlic cloves, minced

1 tablespoon minced ginger

10 oz. ground beef

½ teaspoon kosher salt

½ teaspoon black pepper

2 tablespoons soy sauce

2 teaspoons sesame oil, plus more as needed

Basic Dumpling Wrappers (see page 49)

Water, as needed

Sweet & Spicy Dipping Sauce (see sidebar)

1 Wrap the tofu in cheesecloth and wring the cloth to remove any excess water. Add to the bean sprouts and use a fork to mash the tofu. Add the scallions, onion, garlic, ginger, and ground beef and work the mixture until combined and no large chunks of meat remain. In a small bowl, add the salt, pepper, soy sauce, and the 2 teaspoons of sesame oil and stir to combine. Pour over the meat mixture and gently mix together. Cover the mixture and let rest for 30 minutes.

2 Place a wrapper in the palm of one hand and add 1 tablespoon of the filling. Fold into a half-moon and press down on the edge to seal the dumpling closed. Place the sealed dumplings on a parchment-lined baking sheet and cover with a dry kitchen towel. Repeat until all of the wrappers and filling have been used.

3 Warm a large sauté pan over medium-high heat and lightly coat it with sesame oil. Working in batches, place as many dumplings in the pan as can fit without touching, add 1 cup of water, cover the pan, and cook until the water has evaporated, about 6 minutes. Turn the dumplings over and cook until crispy, about 1 minute. Repeat until all of the dumplings are cooked, adding more sesame oil and water with each batch. Serve immediately with the Sweet & Spicy Dipping Sauce.

Sweet & Spicy Dipping Sauce

INGREDIENTS

¼ cup soy sauce

2 tablespoons rice wine vinegar, plus 2 teaspoons

2 tablespoons water

1½ teaspoons sugar

1 teaspoon sesame oil

1½ teaspoons mashed garlic

½ Fresno chili pepper, seeded and sliced thin

1½ teaspoons sesame seeds, toasted

Reserved scallion greens

1 Place the soy sauce, vinegar, water, and sugar in a mixing bowl and stir until the sugar is dissolved. Add the sesame oil, garlic, and chili pepper and let the mixture sit for 1 hour.

2 Add the sesame seeds and scallion greens, stir to combine, and serve.

Lobster Wontons

YIELD: 4 TO 6 SERVINGS • ACTIVE TIME: 30 MINUTES • TOTAL TIME: 30 MINUTES

A fantastic fusion of Asian and American flavors.

INGREDIENTS

1½ cups minced lobster meat

½ shallot, minced

¼ teaspoon minced ginger

¼ teaspoon minced garlic

1 teaspoon fish sauce

2 tablespoons heavy cream

2 tablespoons chopped chives

Salt and pepper, to taste

24 square Wonton Wrappers (see page 50)

1 egg, beaten

1 Place the lobster meat, shallot, ginger, garlic, fish sauce, heavy cream, chives, salt, and pepper in a mixing bowl and gently fold to combine.

2 Place 1 tablespoon of the mixture in the center of a Wonton Wrapper. Dip a finger into the beaten egg and rub it around the edge of the wrapper. Bring the corners together to make a purse and seal closed. Repeat with the remaining wrappers.

3 Bring water to a boil in a large pot. Working in batches, place the wontons in the boiling water and cook for 3 minutes. Remove and serve immediately.

Seafood Salad Wontons

YIELD: 4 TO 6 SERVINGS • ACTIVE TIME: 30 MINUTES • TOTAL TIME: 30 MINUTES

These were made to nestle into a rich broth. If serving them on their own, try pairing them with a simple aioli.

INGREDIENTS

½ lb. raw shrimp, peeled, deveined, and minced

½ lb. cooked crabmeat, minced

½ shallot, minced

2 tablespoons chopped chives

1 tablespoon fish sauce

2 tablespoons miso

1 tablespoon shrimp paste

¼ cup chopped radish

2 tablespoons sesame seeds, toasted

2 teaspoons sesame oil

2 teaspoons Sherry

24 square Wonton Wrappers (see page 50)

1 egg, beaten

1 Place all of the ingredients, save the wrappers and the egg, in a mixing bowl and gently fold the mixture until combined.

2 Place 2 teaspoons of the mixture in the center of a Wonton Wrapper. Dip a finger into the beaten egg and run it around the edge of the wrapper. Bring the corners together to make a purse and seal it closed. Repeat with the remaining wrappers. Refrigerate until ready to use.

3 Bring water to a boil in a large pot. Working in batches, place the wontons in the boiling water and cook for 3 minutes. Remove and serve immediately.

Pork & Shiitake Gyoza

YIELD: 4 TO 6 SERVINGS • ACTIVE TIME: 30 MINUTES • TOTAL TIME: 45 MINUTES

The emphasis on freshness and umami flavor that Japanese cuisine is famous for are on full display here.

INGREDIENTS

1 cup diced green cabbage

1 teaspoon kosher salt, plus more to taste

1 lb. ground pork

1 garlic clove, minced

4 shiitake mushroom caps, sliced thin

1 tablespoon minced ginger

1 tablespoon soy sauce

2 tablespoons sesame oil

Pepper, to taste

24 round Wonton Wrappers (see page 50)

Water, as needed

Szechuan Peppercorn Oil (see sidebar), for serving

1 Place the cabbage and salt in a mixing bowl, stir to combine, and let sit for 30 minutes. After 30 minutes, squeeze the cabbage to remove as much liquid as possible. Place it in a bowl with the pork, garlic, mushrooms, ginger, soy sauce, and half of the sesame oil and use your hands to combine the mixture. Season with salt and pepper.

2 Place 1 tablespoon of the pork-and-mushroom mixture in the center of a wrapper, wet a finger, and brush it around the wrapper's edge. Fold the wrapper closed and pinch to seal. Repeat with the remaining wrappers.

3 Place the remaining sesame oil in a skillet and warm over medium heat. Place as many gyoza in the pan as will fit without touching. Add 1 cup of water, cover the pan, and cook until the water has evaporated, about 6 minutes. Turn the gyoza over and cook until crispy, about 1 minute. Transfer to a paper towel-lined plate and repeat with any remaining gyoza, replenishing the sesame oil and water as needed. Serve with the Szechuan Peppercorn Oil.

Szechuan Peppercorn Oil

INGREDIENTS

1½ cups vegetable oil

5 star anise pods

1 cinnamon stick

2 bay leaves

3 tablespoons Szechuan peppercorns

¾ cup red pepper flakes

1 teaspoon kosher salt

1 Place the vegetable oil, star anise, cinnamon stick, bay leaves, and Szechuan peppercorns in a skillet and cook over the lowest possible heat for 20 minutes, taking care not to let anything burn.

2 Place the red pepper flakes in a bowl and strain the oil over them. Let cool and then season with salt.

Baozi Dipping Sauce

INGREDIENTS

¼ cup vegetable oil

2 tablespoons minced ginger

2 teaspoons gochugaru or ½ teaspoon red pepper flakes

⅓ cup chinkiang vinegar

1 tablespoon soy sauce, or to taste

1 Place 1 tablespoon of the vegetable oil in a small saucepan and warm over medium heat. Add the ginger, sauté for 2 minutes, and then add the gochugaru and the remaining oil. Let cool.

2 When cool, add the vinegar and soy sauce and place in the refrigerator overnight.

Shengjian Baozi

YIELD: 4 SERVINGS • ACTIVE TIME: 1 HOUR • TOTAL TIME: 2 HOURS

The origin of the steamed pork buns that have won the hearts of foodies all over America.

INGREDIENTS

10 oz. ground pork

1 tablespoon minced ginger

⅓ cup chopped scallions

¼ teaspoon kosher salt

⅛ teaspoon white pepper

1 teaspoon sugar

1 tablespoon soy sauce, plus 1 teaspoon

2 teaspoons rice wine vinegar

2 teaspoons sesame oil

1 tablespoon hot water (125°F), plus more as needed

Baozi Wrappers (see page 54)

¼ cup vegetable oil

Baozi Dipping Sauce (see sidebar), for serving

1 Place the pork, ginger, and scallions in a mixing bowl and stir to combine. Place the remaining ingredients, except for the wrappers and the vegetable oil, in a separate bowl and stir until the salt and sugar have dissolved. Pour the liquid mixture over the pork mixture and stir to incorporate. Cover the mixing bowl and let sit for 30 minutes.

2 Place a wrapper in the palm of one hand and add about 1 tablespoon of the pork mixture. Cup the wrapper and close it over the filling. Squeeze it so that it is tightly sealed and twist to remove any excess dough. Place the filled dumplings, seam-side down, on a parchment-lined baking sheet and let them rise until doubled in size, about 30 minutes.

3 Warm half of the vegetable oil in a skillet over medium heat. Working in batches, add the buns so that they are at least ½" apart. Cook, seam-side up, until golden brown on both sides, 1 to 2 minutes. Add hot water until it is ¼" deep, and hold the cover of the pan in front of you to prevent being harmed by any oil splattering. Cover the pan and cook until the water has evaporated, about 6 minutes. Remove the lid and cook until the bottom is crispy, about 2 minutes. Serve immediately with the dipping sauce.

Har Gow

YIELD: 4 TO 6 SERVINGS • ACTIVE TIME: 1 HOUR • TOTAL TIME: 1½ HOURS

These delicate dumplings are often used to assess the skill of dim sum chefs.

INGREDIENTS

¾ lb. shrimp, peeled and deveined

1½ teaspoons baking soda

2 garlic cloves, minced

2" piece of fresh ginger, minced

1 teaspoon Shaoxing rice wine or dry Sherry

1 teaspoon chili oil

¾ teaspoon kosher salt

½ teaspoon sugar

1 teaspoon cornstarch

Crystal Dumpling Wrappers (see page 53)

Cabbage leaves, for steaming

Chinese black vinegar, for serving (optional)

1 Place the shrimp in a bowl, cover with cold water, and stir in the baking soda. Refrigerate for 30 minutes. Drain the shrimp, rinse under cold water, and pat dry. Slice each shrimp into 5 or 6 pieces. Place in a dry mixing bowl and add the garlic, ginger, rice wine or Sherry, chili oil, salt, sugar, and cornstarch. Stir until thoroughly combined and refrigerate as you prepare the Crystal Dumpling Wrappers.

2 Place a wrapper in the palm of one hand and add about 2 teaspoons of filling. Then, working your way around the edge of the wrapper, create pleats by folding a ¼" section of the wrapper over onto itself and then pinching it closed. When you've made your way around the wrapper, pinch the top of the dumpling closed, so that it resembles a crown. Place on a parchment-lined baking sheet and repeat with the remaining wrappers and filling.

3 Place 1" of water in a large pot and bring it to a boil. Line a steaming tray with the cabbage leaves, place it over the boiling water, and place the dumplings in the steaming tray, leaving ½" between each of the dumplings and also between the dumplings and the edge of the tray. Cover and cook until tender but chewy, about 7 minutes. Transfer to a warmed platter, drizzle the vinegar over the top, and serve immediately.

Chicken & Kimchi Potstickers

YIELD: 4 SERVINGS • ACTIVE TIME: 1½ HOURS • TOTAL TIME: 2 HOURS

Legend has it that these dumplings are the result of a chef forgetting that they were in the wok, an accident that gave them a delightful crispy and golden bottom.

INGREDIENTS

½ lb. ground chicken

1 cup Kimchi (see sidebar), minced

1 tablespoon soy sauce

3" piece of ginger, minced

1½ teaspoons toasted sesame oil

1½ teaspoons Shaoxing rice wine or dry Sherry

1½ teaspoons sugar

1 garlic clove, minced

1 scallion, trimmed and minced

1 tablespoon cornstarch

Basic Dumpling Wrappers (see page 49)

3 tablespoons peanut oil

Szechuan Peppercorn Oil (see page 109), for serving

1 Place the chicken, Kimchi, soy sauce, ginger, sesame oil, rice wine or Sherry, sugar, garlic, and scallion in a mixing bowl and stir until well combined. Sprinkle the cornstarch over the top and stir to incorporate. Cover with plastic wrap and let sit for 30 minutes.

2 Place 1 tablespoon of the filling in the center of a wrapper, wet one finger, and moisten the edge of the wrapper. Fold into a half-moon, squeeze gently to remove as much air as possible, and crimp to seal the edges. Place the sealed dumplings on a parchment-lined baking sheet and repeat with the remaining wrappers and filling.

3 Place 1 tablespoon of the peanut oil in a large skillet and warm over medium-high heat. When it starts to shimmer, add the dumplings in batches and cook until they are golden brown on the bottom. Add 2 tablespoons water, cover, and steam until cooked through, about 4 minutes. Transfer the cooked dumplings to a warmed platter and tent with foil to keep warm. Dry the skillet with a paper towel and repeat until all of the potstickers have been cooked. Serve warm with the Szechuan Peppercorn Oil.

Kimchi

INGREDIENTS

1 head of Napa cabbage, cored and chopped

½ cup kosher salt

2 tablespoons minced ginger

2 tablespoons minced garlic

1 teaspoon sugar

5 tablespoons red pepper flakes

3 bunches of scallions, sliced

Water, as needed

1 Place the cabbage and salt in a large bowl and stir to combine. Wash your hands, or put on gloves, and work the mixture with your hands, squeezing to remove any liquid from the cabbage. Let the mixture rest for 2 hours.

2 Add the remaining ingredients, work the mixture until well combined, and squeeze to remove any liquid. Transfer the mixture to a container and press down so it is tightly packed together. The liquid should be covering the mixture. If it is not, add water until the mixture is covered. Cover the container and let the mixture sit at room temperature for 3 to 7 days, removing the lid daily to release the gas that has built up. This recipe produces about 4 cups of kimchi.

Pork & Roasted Squash Potstickers

YIELD: 6 SERVINGS • ACTIVE TIME: 1½ HOURS • TOTAL TIME: 2 HOURS

These fall-kissed potstickers prove that the dumpling acknowledges no boundary.

INGREDIENTS

2½ lbs. butternut squash, peeled, seeded, and cut into ½" cubes

1 teaspoon coriander seeds

8 whole cloves

½ teaspoon Szechuan peppercorns

½ teaspoon black peppercorns

1 star anise pod

2 cardamom pods, crushed

2 bay leaves

2 cinnamon sticks, crushed

¼ cup vegetable oil

½ lb. ground pork

3 tablespoons minced fresh ginger

3 tablespoons Shaoxing rice wine or dry Sherry

5 tablespoons soy sauce

1 tablespoon toasted sesame oil, plus more for drizzling

3 scallions, minced

1 egg white, lightly beaten

Basic Dumpling Wrappers (see page 49)

Sweet & Spicy Dipping Sauce (see page 103), for serving

Salt, to taste

1 Preheat the oven to 350°F and place the squash in a large mixing bowl. Place the coriander seeds, cloves, peppercorns, star anise, cardamom pods, bay leaves, and cinnamon sticks in a dry skillet and toast until fragrant, 1 to 2 minutes. Grind the mixture into a fine powder using a spice grinder or a mortar and pestle. Add a tablespoon of the spice mixture and a tablespoon of the vegetable oil to the bowl containing the squash, toss to coat, and place the squash on a baking sheet. Place in the oven and roast, while turning over halfway through, until the squash is lightly caramelized and tender, about 30 minutes. Remove from the oven, place in a large mixing bowl, and mash until smooth.

2 While the squash is in the oven, place the ground pork in a large skillet and cook, using a wooden spoon to break it up as it cooks, until completely cooked through, 5 to 7 minutes. Add the cooked pork to the mashed squash and stir to combine. Add the ginger, rice wine or Sherry, soy sauce, sesame oil, scallions, egg white, and another tablespoon of the spice mixture and stir to combine.

3 Place 1 tablespoon of the filling in the center of a wrapper, wet one finger, and moisten the edge of the wrapper. Fold into a half-moon, squeeze gently to remove as much air as possible, and crimp to seal the edges. Place the sealed dumplings on a parchment-lined baking sheet and repeat with the remaining wrappers and filling.

4 Place 1 tablespoon of the vegetable oil in a large skillet and warm over medium-high heat. When it starts to shimmer, add the dumplings in batches and cook until they are golden brown on the bottom. Add 2 tablespoons water, cover, and steam until cooked through, about 4 minutes. Transfer the cooked dumplings to a warmed platter and tent with foil to keep warm. Dry the skillet with a paper towel and repeat until all of the potstickers have been cooked. Serve warm with the Sweet & Spicy Dipping Sauce.

Beef & Cabbage Jiaozi

YIELD: 8 SERVINGS • ACTIVE TIME: 1½ HOURS • TOTAL TIME: 2 HOURS

Assembling, and eating, jiaozi has become an important piece of New Year's celebrations in China.

INGREDIENTS

2 lbs. ground beef

2 tablespoons soy sauce

2" piece of fresh ginger, minced

2 tablespoons cinnamon

2 teaspoons sugar

Salt and pepper, to taste

1 lb. cabbage leaves, blanched and minced

6 scallion whites, minced

Basic Dumpling Wrappers (see page 49)

Cilantro, chopped, for garnish

Sweet & Spicy Dipping Sauce (see page 103), for serving

1 Place the ground beef, soy sauce, ginger, cinnamon, sugar, salt, and pepper in a mixing bowl and stir to combine. Cover with plastic wrap and let stand for 30 minutes. After 30 minutes, add the minced cabbage and scallion whites to the mixture, place a small amount in a skillet, and cook until cooked through. Taste and adjust the seasoning if necessary.

2 Place 1 tablespoon of the filling in the center of a wrapper, wet one finger, and moisten the edge of the wrapper. Pinch one-quarter of the wrapper and fold it over itself to create a pleat. Pinch to seal and then repeat with the rest of the wrapper, so that the sealed dumpling resembles a rose about to bloom. Place the sealed dumplings on a parchment-lined baking sheet and repeat with the remaining wrappers and filling.

3 Bring a large pot of water to a boil. Carefully add the dumplings. Once the water resumes boiling, add a cup of cold water to keep it at a gentle boil. If necessary, continue adding cold water to keep the water at a gentle boil. Once the dumplings start to float to the surface, cook for another 5 to 6 minutes. Garnish with cilantro and serve immediately with the Sweet & Spicy Dipping Sauce.

Siu Mai

YIELD: 6 TO 8 SERVINGS • ACTIVE TIME: 45 MINUTES • TOTAL TIME: 1 HOUR

These dainty, open-faced dumplings are a must any time you find yourself out for dim sum.

INGREDIENTS

8 shiitake mushroom caps, chopped

1 chicken bouillon cube

¾ lb. ground pork

½ lb. shrimp, peeled, deveined, and minced

4 scallion whites, sliced thin, plus more for garnish

¼ red bell pepper, seeded and minced

2 egg whites

1 tablespoon soy sauce

1 tablespoon Shaoxing rice wine or dry Sherry

1 teaspoon fish sauce

1 teaspoon toasted sesame oil

2 teaspoons cornstarch

½ teaspoon sugar

½ teaspoon white pepper

36 round Wonton Wrappers (see page 50)

Cabbage leaves, for steaming

Carrots, peeled and minced, for garnish

Crab roe, for garnish

1 Place the chopped mushrooms in a bowl and then crush the bouillon cube. Add it to the bowl along with the pork, shrimp, scallion whites, red pepper, egg whites, soy sauce, rice wine or Sherry, fish sauce, sesame oil, cornstarch, sugar, and white pepper and stir until well combined.

2 Place a wrapper in a cupped hand and fill it with enough of the pork-and-shrimp mixture to fill the wrapper to the top. Flatten the filling with a butter knife and gently tighten the wrapper around the filling, forming a rough cylindrical shape with a flat bottom. Place the filled dumplings on a parchment-lined baking sheet and repeat with the remaining wrappers and filling.

3 Place 1" of water in a large pot and bring it to a boil. Line a steaming tray with the cabbage leaves and then add the siu mai, leaving ½" between each of the dumplings and also between the dumplings and the edge of the tray. Place the steaming tray over the boiling water, cover, and steam until the dumplings are cooked through, tender, and still chewy, about 10 minutes. Transfer the cooked dumplings to a warmed platter and top with the additional scallion whites, the carrots, and a bit of crab roe.

Momos

YIELD: 4 SERVINGS • ACTIVE TIME: 45 MINUTES • TOTAL TIME: 1½ HOURS

The meat of choice in Tibet, where these dumplings are beloved, is yak, but ground beef or lamb will also work.

INGREDIENTS

¾ lb. ground beef

3 garlic cloves, minced

½ large yellow onion, minced

5 scallion whites, sliced thin

2" piece of ginger, minced

Salt, to taste

¾ teaspoon Szechuan peppercorns

2 tablespoons safflower or peanut oil

5 tablespoons water

Basic Dumpling Wrappers (see page 49)

Cabbage leaves, for steaming (optional)

Sweet & Spicy Dipping Sauce (see page 103), for serving

1 Place the ground beef, garlic, onion, scallion whites, ginger, and a couple pinches of salt in a mixing bowl and stir to combine. Place the Szechuan peppercorns in a small dry skillet and toast over medium heat until fragrant, 2 to 3 minutes. Using a spice grinder or a mortar and pestle, crush the peppercorns into a fine powder. Place the powder in a bowl, add the oil, water, and a couple of pinches of salt and stir to combine. Pour over the ground beef mixture and stir to incorporate.

2 Place a wrapper in a cupped hand and place about 1 tablespoon of filling in the center, leaving about ¾" of open wrapper around the edge. Moisten the edge with a wet finger, fold the wrapper into a half-moon, and press down to seal, trying to remove as much air as possible. To pleat the sealed edge, make small folds in the wrapper and press them flat as you work along the edge. Place the sealed dumpling on a parchment-lined baking sheet and repeat with the remaining wrappers and filling.

3 Place 1" of water in a large pot and bring it to a boil. Line a steaming tray with the cabbage leaves and then add the momos in batches, leaving ½" between each of the dumplings and also between the dumplings and the edge of the tray. Place the steaming tray over the boiling water, cover, and steam until the dumplings have puffed up slightly and become slightly translucent, about 8 minutes. Transfer to a warmed plate, tent loosely with foil to keep warm, and repeat with the remaining dumplings. Serve immediately with the Sweet & Spicy Dipping Sauce.

Bansh

YIELD: 4 SERVINGS • ACTIVE TIME: 1½ HOURS • TOTAL TIME: 2 HOURS

In Mongolia, you'd find the stronger tasting mutton in these small dumplings, which are so delicious no dipping sauce is required.

INGREDIENTS

¾ lb. ground lamb

1 yellow onion, minced

2 large garlic gloves, minced

1 tablespoon ground coriander

Handful of parsley leaves, minced

Salt and pepper, to taste

3 to 5 teaspoons water

Basic Dumpling Wrappers (see page 49)

Cucumber, sliced thin, for serving

Radish, sliced thin, for serving

1 Place the lamb, onion, garlic, coriander, parsley, salt, and pepper in a mixing bowl and stir to combine. Place a small piece of the mixture in a skillet and cook it through. Taste and adjust seasoning if necessary. Add the water 1 teaspoon at a time and stir until the filling is smooth.

2 Cup a wrapper in a hand and add about a teaspoon of filling. Wet a finger and moisten the edge of the wrapper. Pinch one-quarter of the wrapper and fold it over itself to create a pleat. Pinch to seal and then repeat with the rest of the wrapper, so that the sealed dumpling resembles a rose about to bloom. Place the sealed dumplings on a parchment-lined baking sheet and repeat with the remaining wrappers and filling.

3 Bring a large pot of salted water to a boil and add the dumplings. Cook, while stirring to prevent sticking, until the dumplings float to the surface, 8 to 10 minutes. Place the cooked dumplings on a warm platter and serve with the cucumber and radish.

Crab Rangoons

YIELD: 6 SERVINGS • ACTIVE TIME: 25 MINUTES • TOTAL TIME: 45 MINUTES

Once these have been fried, do try and hold off devouring them until they've cooled slightly, as the filling can be seriously hot.

INGREDIENTS

For the Spicy Pineapple Sauce

½ cup chopped fresh pineapple

2 garlic cloves

½ red bell pepper, seeded and chopped

¼ teaspoon red pepper flakes, or to taste

1 cup distilled white vinegar

¾ cup sugar

¼ cup water

For the Rangoons

2 (8 oz.) packages of cream cheese, at room temperature

6 oz. fresh crabmeat

2 tablespoons confectioners' sugar

¼ teaspoon kosher salt

40 square Wonton Wrappers (see page 50)

Peanut or grapeseed oil, for frying

1 To prepare the sauce, place the pineapple, garlic, bell pepper, and red pepper flakes in a food processor or blender and pulse until minced. Pour the mixture into a small saucepan and add the vinegar, sugar, and water. Bring to a boil over medium heat, reduce to a simmer, and cook until the sauce thickens and becomes shiny, 10 to 12 minutes. Remove from the heat and let cool before serving.

2 To prepare the rangoons, place the cream cheese, crabmeat, sugar, and salt in a medium bowl and fold to combine. Place about 1 tablespoon of the filling in the middle of a wrapper. Rub the wrapper's edge with a wet finger, bring the corners together, pinch to seal tightly, and transfer to a parchment-lined baking sheet. Repeat with the remaining wrappers and filling.

3 Add oil to a Dutch oven until it is 2" deep and bring to 325°F over medium heat. Working in batches of six to eight, gently slip the wontons into the hot oil and fry, while turning, until golden all over, about 1 minute per side. Transfer the cooked rangoons to a paper towel-lined wire rack and repeat with the remaining dumplings. Let cool briefly before serving with the sauce.

Chicken Gyoza

YIELD: 4 TO 6 SERVINGS • ACTIVE TIME: 25 MINUTES • TOTAL TIME: 40 MINUTES

Adapted from one of the standards that Chef Ming Tsai built his glittering reputation upon.

INGREDIENTS

- 2 cups shredded Napa cabbage
- 1 teaspoon kosher salt
- ⅓ lb. ground chicken
- 1 tablespoon minced fresh ginger
- 1 carrot, peeled and shredded
- 2 scallions, trimmed and chopped
- 2 garlic cloves, minced
- 2 tablespoons soy sauce
- 2 teaspoons sesame oil
- 1 tablespoon sesame seeds
- Large pinch of red pepper flakes
- ½ egg, lightly beaten
- 30 round Wonton Wrappers (see page 50)
- 3 tablespoons vegetable oil
- Water, as needed

1 Place the cabbage, salt, ground chicken, ginger, carrot, scallions, and garlic in a large bowl and stir until thoroughly combined. Add the soy sauce, sesame oil, sesame seeds, red pepper flakes, and egg and stir to incorporate.

2 Spoon 2 teaspoons of the filling into the center of a wrapper and run a wet finger along the wrapper's edge. Fold into a half-moon and press down on the edge to seal. Repeat until all of the filling and wrappers have been used.

3 Place a large skillet over medium-high heat and add 1 tablespoon of the vegetable oil. Place as many gyoza in the pan as will fit without touching. Add about ½ cup of water, cover the pan, and cook until the water has evaporated, about 6 minutes. Turn the gyoza over and cook until crispy, about 1 minute. Transfer to a paper towel-lined plate and repeat with any remaining gyoza, replenishing the oil and water as needed. Serve immediately.

INGREDIENTS

For the Dough

2¾ cups bread flour, plus more for dusting

½ cup water

1 teaspoon kosher salt

1 egg

For the Filling

½ lb. ground pork

½ lb. ground beef

2 small onions, minced

1 teaspoon kosher salt, plus more to taste

¼ teaspoon ground black pepper

1 egg, beaten

1 tablespoon water

4 tablespoons unsalted butter

For Serving

Sour cream

Dill, chopped

Malt vinegar (optional)

Pelmeni

YIELD: 4 SERVINGS • ACTIVE TIME: 1 HOUR • TOTAL TIME: 2 HOURS

Bearing a similar look to an Italian tortellini, serve this Russian delicacy with sour cream and freshly chopped dill.

1 To prepare the dough, sift the flour into a mixing bowl, add the remaining ingredients, and work the mixture until it holds together. Place the dough on a flour-dusted work surface and knead until it is firm and smooth, about 5 minutes. Cover in plastic wrap and place in the refrigerator for 1 hour. After 1 hour, roll out the dough on a flour-dusted work surface until it can fit through the widest setting on a pasta maker. Feed the dough through the machine, adjusting the settings to reduce the thickness with each pass, until you can see a hand through the dough. With a ring cutter or mason jar, cut the dough into as many 3" circles as you can, place them on a parchment-lined baking sheet, and cover with a kitchen towel.

2 To prepare the filling, place the ground pork, ground beef, onions, salt, and pepper in a mixing bowl and stir to combine. Place the egg and water in a bowl and beat to combine. Brush the edge of a dough circle with the egg wash, place 1 tablespoon of the filling in the center, and fold the edges together. Seal, brush the tips of the dumpling with more of the egg wash, bring them together, and crimp to seal.

3 Bring a pot of salted water to a boil. When it is boiling, reduce the heat to medium, add the pelmeni, and cook for 8 minutes. When the pelmeni are almost cooked, place the butter in a skillet and melt it over medium heat. Add the cooked pelmeni, toss to coat, and serve with the sour cream, chopped dill, and malt vinegar, if desired.

Khinkali

YIELD: 4 TO 6 SERVINGS • ACTIVE TIME: 1 HOUR • TOTAL TIME: 2 HOURS

If these lovely pockets are any indication, the people in the nation of Georgia eat very well.

INGREDIENTS

For the Dough

4 cups all-purpose flour, plus more for dusting

1½ teaspoons kosher salt

1¼ cups warm water (105°F)

For the Filling

¾ lb. ground pork

¾ lb. ground beef

¼ cup chopped cilantro leaves

2 teaspoons dried fenugreek leaves

1 teaspoon red pepper flakes

2 large onions, minced

Salt and pepper, to taste

1 To prepare the dough, place all of the ingredients in a mixing bowl and stir until the dough holds together. Place the dough on a flour-dusted work surface and knead until smooth, about 5 minutes. Cover in plastic wrap and place in the refrigerator for 1 hour.

2 To prepare the filling, place all of the ingredients in a large bowl and stir until well combined.

3 Place the dough on a flour-dusted work surface, divide it into 24 pieces, and roll them out into 5" circles. Place a circle in the palm of one hand, place 2½ tablespoons of the filling in the center, and fold the edges together. Use your other hand to pinch the dumpling closed and then twist it to form a knot on top. Repeat with the remaining dumplings.

4 Bring salted water to a boil in a large pot. Working in batches, add the dumplings to the boiling water and cook until they float to the surface and the dough is tender, about 10 minutes. Serve immediately.

Pyzy

YIELD: 4 TO 6 SERVINGS • ACTIVE TIME: 40 MINUTES • TOTAL TIME: 1 HOUR

A quick, unfilled version of the traditional Ukranian dumpling.

1 Bring a large pot of salted water to a boil. Cut half of the potatoes into chunks and add these chunks to the boiling water. Cook until fork-tender, drain, and transfer to a large bowl. Mash until smooth and set aside.

2 While half of the potatoes are cooking, grate the remaining potatoes onto a kitchen towel. Wring to remove as much liquid as possible and then place them in a bowl with the mashed potatoes. Add the eggs and the flours, season with salt, and stir until the dough is no longer sticky and holds its shape when squeezed. If it's too sticky, incorporate more all-purpose flour in 1-tablespoon increments. Roll tablespoons of the dough into spheres that are slightly larger than golf balls.

3 Place the bacon and onion in a skillet and cook over medium heat until the onion is golden brown and the bacon is crispy, about 12 minutes. Remove from heat and cover the pan.

4 While the bacon and onion are cooking, bring another large pot of salted water to a boil. Working in batches of 4 or 5, add the dumplings to the boiling water and cook until they float to the surface, about 4 minutes. Taste one for doneness. You should not taste the flour if cooked properly. Either cook longer or remove and place in a colander to drain. When all of the dumplings have been cooked, place them on a warmed platter and top with the bacon-and-onion mixture.

INGREDIENTS

Salt, to taste

2½ lbs. russet potatoes, peeled

2 large eggs, beaten

1 cup all-purpose flour, plus more as needed

1 tablespoon potato flour

6 oz. thick-cut bacon, chopped

1 large yellow onion, sliced thin

Zazharka & Mushroom Varenyky

YIELD: 6 TO 8 SERVINGS • ACTIVE TIME: 45 MINUTES • TOTAL TIME: 1½ HOURS

Zazharka would typically go on top of these dumplings, but we feel it's too tasty to not be granted inside access.

INGREDIENTS

9 tablespoons unsalted butter

½ lb. cremini mushrooms, rinsed well and minced

2 small yellow onions, minced

2 garlic cloves, minced

Salt, to taste

6 oz. bacon, minced

Pierogi Wrappers (see page 61)

1 tablespoon vegetable oil

Sour cream, for serving

1 Place 3 tablespoons of the butter in a large skillet and melt it over medium heat. When it has melted and stopped foaming, add the mushrooms, one of the onions, the garlic, and a few pinches of salt and cook, while stirring occasionally, until they become very soft and brown, about 20 minutes. Transfer the mixture to a bowl and wipe out the skillet.

2 Place the bacon in the skillet and cook over medium heat until the fat starts to render, about 2 minutes. Add the remaining onion, season with salt, and reduce the heat to medium-low. Cook, while stirring occasionally, until the onion is golden brown, about 20 minutes. Add the remaining butter, stir until it is melted, and add this mixture to the mushroom mixture. Stir to combine and let the mixture cool completely.

3 Hold a wrapper in the palm of one hand and place 1 teaspoon of filling in the center. Fold the wrapper into a half-moon, squeeze to remove as much air as possible, and pinch to seal it tightly. Repeat with the remaining wrappers and filling.

4 Bring salted water to a boil in a large pot. Add the vegetable oil and then, working in batches, use a slotted spoon to gently lower the varenyky into the water. Gently stir to keep them from sticking to the bottom. Once they float to the surface, cook for another 3 minutes. Transfer the cooked dumplings to a warmed platter and tent with foil to keep warm. When all of the dumplings have been cooked, top with any remaining filling and serve with sour cream.

Stuffed Matzo Balls

YIELD: 4 TO 6 SERVINGS • ACTIVE TIME: 45 MINUTES • TOTAL TIME: 1½ HOURS

A break from tradition, yes. But that's no reason to pass over these dumplings.

INGREDIENTS

2 tablespoons olive oil

1 large onion, diced

6 oz. chicken liver, minced

Salt and pepper, to taste

Dough from Matzo Balls (see page 36)

1 Place half of the oil in a skillet and warm over medium heat. Add the onion and cook until it starts to soften, about 5 minutes. Add the chicken liver, season with salt and pepper, and cook, while stirring, until the chicken liver is cooked through, about 3 minutes. Remove the pan from heat and let the mixture cool. When it has cooled completely, transfer to a cutting board and mince. Form the mixture into balls and place them in the freezer for 15 minutes.

2 Roll tablespoons of the dough into balls and place a ball in one of your palms. Flatten it and then place one of the chicken liver balls in the center. Shape the dough around the filling and then roll into a smooth sphere. Repeat with the remaining balls of dough and chicken liver mixture.

3 Place the remaining oil in the skillet and warm over medium heat. When it starts to shimmer, add the stuffed matzo balls and cook, while turning occasionally, until they are golden brown all over. Serve by themselves or add to a simmering soup.

Kroppkakor

YIELD: 4 SERVINGS • ACTIVE TIME: 30 MINUTES • TOTAL TIME: 1 HOUR

Traditionally the filling is only seasoned with allspice, but in the interest of balance and nuance, we've made a few additions.

INGREDIENTS

- 1 lb. bacon, cut into small cubes
- 2 yellow onions, diced
- ½ teaspoon ground allspice
- ½ teaspoon ground cloves
- ½ teaspoon ground cardamom
- ½ teaspoon ground nutmeg
- Salt and pepper, to taste
- Kroppkakor Wrappers (see page 58)
- Lingonberry jam or black currant jelly, for serving

1 Place the bacon in a large skillet and cook over medium heat for 5 minutes in order to render the fat. Add the onions, reduce the heat to low, and cook until they have softened. Add the seasonings and cook until the bacon is crispy, about 5 minutes. Remove from heat and let cool. When cool, place the mixture in a food processor and blitz until pureed.

2 Place 2 tablespoons in the center of a wrapper and shape the dough around the filling to form a ball. Repeat until all of the filling and wrappers have been used.

3 Fill a large pot two-thirds of the way with salted water and bring to a rolling boil. Carefully drop the balls into the boiling water, cook until they float to the top, and serve with the lingonberry jam or black currant jelly.

Pitepalt

YIELD: 8 SERVINGS • ACTIVE TIME: 1 HOUR • TOTAL TIME: 2 HOURS

Kroppkakor's cousin from the north, this hearty Swedish dumpling will serve you well on a frigid day.

INGREDIENTS

¾ lb. pork belly, skin removed and diced

½ tablespoon olive oil, plus more as needed

Leaves from 1 sprig of rosemary, minced

2 lbs. russet potatoes, peeled

2 cups all-purpose flour, plus more as needed

1½ tablespoons kosher salt, plus more to taste

6 tablespoons unsalted butter, melted and warm

Lingonberry jam or black currant jelly, for serving

1 Bring water to a boil in a small saucepan. Add the pork belly and cook for 5 minutes. Remove, transfer to a paper towel-lined plate, and pat the pork belly dry. Place the olive oil in a large skillet, warm over medium-low heat, and then add half of the pork belly. Cook, while stirring occasionally, until the pieces are browned all over, about 10 minutes. Place the pieces in a bowl and repeat with the remaining pork belly, adding more oil if the pan starts to look dry. Add the rosemary to the bowl, stir to combine, and set the mixture aside.

2 Grate the potatoes into a large bowl of cold water. Soak for 5 minutes and drain. Add the flour and salt to the potatoes and work the mixture until a thick dough forms. Shape the mixture into golf ball-sized spheres and make a deep indentation in each one. Fill with some of the pork belly mixture and smooth the dough over the filling. Repeat until all of the balls have been filled.

3 Bring a large pot of salted water to a boil. Use a slotted spoon to gently lower the dumplings into the water, gently stir to keep them from sticking, reduce the heat so that the water gently boils, and cook for 45 minutes. Place the cooked dumplings on a warmed platter, top with the melted butter and any remaining filling, and serve with the lingonberry jam or black currant jelly.

Runzas

YIELD: 4 SERVINGS • ACTIVE TIME: 30 MINUTES • TOTAL TIME: 2 HOURS

These hearty dumplings are a staple at German Oktoberfest celebrations, and have also become a favorite in the American Midwest.

INGREDIENTS

For the Dough

¾ cup warm water (110°F)

1 teaspoon active dry yeast

½ cup sweetened condensed milk

¼ cup vegetable oil

2 tablespoons sugar

1 large egg

3½ cups all-purpose flour, plus more for dusting

1 teaspoon kosher salt

For the Filling

6 tablespoons unsalted butter

1½ lbs. ground beef

1 yellow onion, minced

2½ cups chopped green cabbage

Salt and pepper, to taste

For Serving

Sauerkraut

1 To prepare the dough, place the water and yeast in the mixing bowl of a stand mixer and let it stand until it is foamy, about 5 minutes. Fit the stand mixer with the dough hook, add the remaining ingredients, and mix on low speed until the dough just holds together. Increase the speed to medium and mix until the dough is a ball and no longer sticks to the side of the mixing bowl. Cover with a damp cloth and let rest until the dough doubles in size, about 1 hour.

2 To prepare the filling, place 1 tablespoon of the butter in a large skillet and melt over medium-high heat. Add the ground beef and cook, while using a wooden spoon to break it up, until it is browned, about 5 minutes. Place the meat on a paper towel-lined plate to drain, wipe out the skillet, and add another tablespoon of butter. Melt over medium heat, add the onion, and cook until it is tender. Add the cabbage and cook until it starts to wilt. Return the meat to the pan, stir to combine, and season with salt and pepper. Remove from heat and let the mixture cool.

3 Place the dough on a flour-dusted work surface, cut it into eight pieces, and roll each one into a 6" circle. Place a dough circle into a lightly flour-dusted bowl, place about ¾ cup of the cooled filling in the center, fold the dough over it, and crimp to seal. Place the buns, seam-side down, on a parchment-lined baking sheet, cover with plastic wrap, and let them rise for 30 minutes.

4 Preheat the oven to 350°F. Place the buns in the oven and cook for 10 minutes. Melt the remaining butter in a skillet and set it aside. After 10 minutes, remove the baking sheet from the oven and brush the top of each bun with some of the melted butter. Return to the oven and bake until golden brown, about 10 minutes. Remove, brush with any remaining butter, and serve with the sauerkraut.

Cornish Pasties

YIELD: 6 SERVINGS • ACTIVE TIME: 30 MINUTES
TOTAL TIME: 1 HOUR AND 15 MINUTES

These pockets came to prominence thanks to the miners in Cornwall, who loved that they remained warm as they labored.

INGREDIENTS

For the Dough

3 cups all-purpose flour, plus more for dusting

¾ teaspoon kosher salt

½ cup lard or unsalted butter, cut into small pieces

1 large egg, beaten

¼ cup cold water, plus more as needed

2 teaspoons distilled white vinegar

For the Filling

¾ lb. skirt steak, cut into ½" cubes

¼ cup peeled and chopped parsnips

¼ cup peeled and chopped turnips

1 small onion, chopped

1 cup peeled and chopped potato

1 tablespoon fresh thyme leaves, chopped

2 tablespoons tomato paste

Salt and pepper, to taste

1 large egg, beaten

1 tablespoon water

1 To prepare the dough, place the flour and salt in a bowl, add the lard or butter, and use a pastry blender to work the mixture until coarse crumbs form. Beat the egg, water, and vinegar together in a separate bowl and then drizzle this mixture over the flour mixture. Use the pastry blender to work the mixture until it starts to come together. Knead the dough with your hands, adding more water in 1-teaspoon increments if it is too dry. Cut the dough into 6 pieces, cover with plastic wrap, and chill in the refrigerator.

2 Preheat the oven to 400°F and prepare the filling. Place all of the ingredients, except for the egg and water, in a bowl and stir to combine. Place the egg and water in a separate bowl and beat to combine.

3 Place the pieces of dough on a flour-dusted work surface, roll them into 8" circles, and place ½ cup of the filling in the center of each pastry. Brush the edge of each circle with water and fold each one into a half-moon. Crimp to seal and place the sealed pastries on a parchment-lined baking sheet.

4 Place the egg and water in a small bowl and beat to combine. Brush the pastries with the egg wash and use a paring knife to make a small incision in the side of each one. Bake in the oven for 15 minutes, reduce the temperature to 350°F, and bake for another 25 minutes. Remove from oven and let cool on a wire rack before serving.

Papas Rellenas

YIELD: 4 TO 6 SERVINGS • ACTIVE TIME: 30 MINUTES • TOTAL TIME: 1 HOUR

These crispy, stuffed potato balls are a classic of Cuban cuisine.

INGREDIENTS

3 lbs. potatoes, peeled and chopped

1 garlic clove, minced

2 teaspoons kosher salt

1 teaspoon black pepper

1 tablespoon vegetable oil, plus more for frying

1 small green bell pepper, seeded and minced

1 yellow onion, minced

½ lb. ground beef

2 tablespoons tomato paste

¼ cup green olives, pitted and sliced

¼ cup raisins

½ teaspoon paprika

2 eggs, lightly beaten

½ cup bread crumbs

1 Bring water to a boil in a large pan. Add the potatoes, cover, and cook until fork-tender, about 25 minutes. Drain the potatoes, place them in a large bowl, and mash until smooth. Add the garlic and half of the salt and pepper and stir to incorporate.

2 Warm the vegetable oil in a skillet over medium heat. When the oil starts to shimmer, add the pepper and onion and cook until the onion is translucent, about 5 minutes. Add the ground beef and cook, while using a wooden spoon to break it up, until it is cooked through. Add the tomato paste, olives, raisins, the remaining salt and pepper, and the paprika and cook for 2 minutes. Transfer the mixture to a paper towel-lined baking sheet and let it drain.

3 Add vegetable oil to a Dutch oven until it is 2" deep and bring it to 375°F. Place the eggs and bread crumbs in two separate bowls. Place 2 tablespoons of the potato mixture in one hand, pat it flat, and then place a tablespoon of the ground beef mixture in the center. Shape the potato around the filling to create a ball and dip the ball into the egg. Roll the ball in the bread crumbs until coated and place on a parchment-lined baking sheet. Repeat until all of the potato mixture and ground beef mixture have been used up.

4 Place the balls in the hot oil and cook until golden brown, about 2 minutes. Remove with a slotted spoon and set them on a paper towel-lined plate to drain.

Empanadas

YIELD: 4 SERVINGS • ACTIVE TIME: 45 MINUTES • TOTAL TIME: 1½ HOURS

This particular recipe features pork, but this crowd favorite can incorporate a variety of meats and other ingredients.

INGREDIENTS

For the Dough

¼ teaspoon kosher salt

6 tablespoons warm water (110°F)

1½ cups all-purpose flour, plus more for dusting

3 tablespoons lard or unsalted butter, cut into small pieces

For the Filling

2 teaspoons vegetable oil, plus more for frying

1 yellow onion, minced

1 garlic clove, minced

¾ lb. ground pork

1 (14 oz.) can of crushed tomatoes

½ teaspoon kosher salt

¼ teaspoon black pepper

1 cinnamon stick

2 whole cloves

2 tablespoons raisins

2 teaspoons apple cider vinegar

2 tablespoons slivered almonds, toasted

1 To prepare the dough, dissolve the salt in the warm water. Place the flour in a mixing bowl, add the lard, and work the mixture with a pastry blender until the mixture is crumbly. Add the salted water and knead the mixture until a stiff dough forms. Cut the dough into eight pieces, cover them with plastic wrap, and place in the refrigerator for 20 minutes.

2 To prepare the filling, place the vegetable oil in a skillet and warm over medium heat. Add the onion and cook until soft, about 5 minutes. Add the garlic, cook for 2 minutes, and then add the ground pork. Cook, while breaking the pork up with a spoon, until light brown, about 5 minutes. Drain off any excess fat and add the tomatoes, salt, pepper, cinnamon stick, cloves, raisins, and vinegar. Simmer until the filling is thick, about 30 minutes. Remove from heat and let cool before folding in the toasted almonds.

3 Add vegetable oil to a Dutch oven until it is 2" deep and bring it to 350°F. Preheat the oven to 200°F and place a platter in the oven. Place the dough on a flour-dusted work surface and roll each piece into a 5" circle. Place 3 tablespoons of the filling in the center of a circle, brush the edge of the circle with water, and fold into a half-moon. Press down on the edge to seal the empanada tight, trying to remove as much air as possible. Repeat with the remaining pieces of dough and filling.

4 Working in two batches, place the empanadas in the hot oil and fry until golden brown, about 5 minutes. Drain on paper towels and then place them in the warm oven while you cook the next batch.

Garden Variety

Mother Nature gives us so much that at times it can be difficult to know what to do with it all. Fortunately, dumplings are an ideal solution to this exciting predicament. One of the few preparations that can be counted upon to contain the Earth's ample bounty, dumplings filled with vegetables and herbs offer a variety of flavors that is not frequently matched.

From the Punjabi Samosa (see page 156) that is as beloved as any dumpling to Mandu filled with tangy and spicy kimchi and the cheese-laden decadence of the Tiropitakia (see page 171), even those who strongly believe that the role of a dumpling is to encase a savory meat filling will find plenty to love in these vegetarian stuffed dumplings.

Punjabi Samosa

YIELD: 4 SERVINGS • ACTIVE TIME: 45 MINUTES • TOTAL TIME: 1½ HOURS

The Cilantro Chutney is a beautiful counterbalance to the delicate spice of the filling.

INGREDIENTS

2 russet potatoes, peeled and chopped

2 tablespoons vegetable oil, plus more for frying

1 teaspoon coriander seeds, crushed

½ teaspoon fennel seeds, crushed

Pinch of fenugreek seeds, crushed

1 tablespoon minced ginger

1 teaspoon minced garlic

1 teaspoon seeded and minced jalapeño pepper

2 teaspoons chili powder

2 tablespoons ground coriander

¾ teaspoon turmeric

1 tablespoon amchoor powder

½ teaspoon garam masala

6 curry leaves, minced

Salt, to taste

Samosa Wrappers (see page 57)

Cilantro Chutney (see page 165), for serving

1 Place the potatoes in a saucepan and cover with water. Bring the water to a boil and cook until fork-tender, about 20 minutes. Transfer to a bowl, mash until smooth, and set aside.

2 Place the oil in a skillet and warm over medium heat. Add the crushed seeds and cook until fragrant, about 2 minutes. Add the ginger, garlic, and jalapeño, stir-fry for 2 minutes, and then add the chili powder, coriander, turmeric, amchoor powder, and garam masala and cook for another minute before adding the mashed potatoes and the curry leaves. Stir to combine, season with salt, transfer the mixture to a bowl, and let it cool.

3 Add vegetable oil to a Dutch oven until it is 2″ deep and heat it to 325°F over medium heat. When the mixture has cooled, brush the flat edge of each Samosa Wrapper with water. Fold one corner of the flat edge toward the other to make a cone and then pinch to seal. Fill each cone one-third of the way with the potato filling, brush the opening with water, and pinch until sealed. Place the sealed samosas on a parchment-lined baking sheet.

4 When all of the wrappers have been filled, add them to the hot oil in batches and fry, while stirring and turning them over occasionally, until they are golden brown, about 5 minutes. Transfer the cooked samosas to a paper towel-lined plate and serve with the Cilantro Chutney once they have all been cooked.

Herb Chutney

INGREDIENTS

1 cup cilantro leaves, chopped

½ cup mint leaves

4 garlic cloves

1 teaspoon seeded and minced jalapeño pepper

1 small yellow onion, chopped

¼ cup tamarind pulp

Water, as needed

Salt, to taste

Place the herbs, garlic, jalapeño, onion, and tamarind pulp in a food processor and puree until smooth, adding water if the mixture is too thick. Season with salt and refrigerate until ready to serve.

Dal Fara

YIELD: 4 SERVINGS • ACTIVE TIME: 30 MINUTES • TOTAL TIME: 24 HOURS

This popular snack in India is typically made with split peas, but this version capitalizes on the wonderful nutty flavor of chickpeas.

INGREDIENTS

For the Filling

1½ cups dried chickpeas

2 tablespoons water

2" piece of ginger, chopped

½ cup cilantro leaves

½ jalapeño pepper, seeded and minced

1 teaspoon cumin seeds

Pinch of hing powder (optional)

Salt, to taste

For the Dough

3 cups rice flour, plus more as needed

Salt, to taste

4 teaspoons vegetable oil

Warm water (105°F), as needed

For Serving

Herb Chutney (see sidebar)

1 Start preparations for the filling the night before you plan to serve the dal fara. Place the chickpeas in a mixing bowl, cover with water, and soak overnight. The next day, drain the chickpeas and place in a food processor with the remaining ingredients. Puree until smooth and set aside.

2 To prepare the dough, place the rice flour and a pinch of salt in a mixing bowl, stir to combine, and then add the oil. Stir to incorporate and gradually add water until the dough just holds together. Take care not to overwork the mixture. Cover the bowl with a damp cloth and let it rest for 20 minutes.

3 Place the dough on a flour-dusted work surface and divide it into 16 pieces. Roll the pieces into balls, lightly moisten your hands, place a ball of dough in one hand, and flatten it into a 3" round that is ⅛" thick. Place 1 tablespoon of filling in the center of the round, fold into a half-moon, and pinch the edge to seal the dumpling. Repeat with the remaining balls of dough and filling.

4 Bring a large pot of salted water to a boil. Working in batches, place the dumplings in the water and stir to ensure they don't stick to the bottom. Once they rise to the surface, cook for another 2 minutes. Remove with a slotted spoon, transfer to a warm platter, and tent with foil to keep warm. When all of the dumplings have been cooked, serve with the Herb Chutney.

Chai Kuih

YIELD: 4 SERVINGS • ACTIVE TIME: 1 HOUR • TOTAL TIME: 2 HOURS

These "vegetable cakes" are a popular street food in a number of Chinese cities.

INGREDIENTS

2 tablespoons peanut or grapeseed oil

1 lb. jicama, peeled and grated

¼ cup minced shiitake mushroom caps

1 carrot, peeled and finely grated

2 tablespoons soy sauce

1 teaspoon sugar

Salt and pepper, to taste

Crystal Dumpling Wrappers (see page 53)

Cabbage leaves, for steaming

Chili sauce or Szechuan Peppercorn Oil (see page 109), for serving

1 Place the oil in a wok or large skillet and warm over low heat. When the oil begins to shimmer, add the jicama, mushrooms, and carrot and cook, while stirring frequently, until the jicama is tender but still crunchy, about 15 minutes. Add the soy sauce and sugar, season with salt and pepper, and stir to combine. Remove from heat and let the mixture cool.

2 Line a baking sheet with parchment paper. Place 1 tablespoon of the jicama mixture in the center of a wrapper. Moisten the wrapper's edge with a wet finger and fold the wrapper over to create a triangle. Take the far edge of the wrapper and gently fold it over the filling to meet the other edge. Using your thumb and index finger, pinch both edges together to create a tight seal, trying to remove as much air as you can. Place the filled dumplings on the baking sheet and repeat with the remaining wrappers and filling.

3 Place 1" of water in a saucepan and bring it to a boil. Line a steaming tray with the cabbage leaves and place the dumplings in the tray, leaving ½" between each of the dumplings and also between the dumplings and the edge of the tray. Place the tray over the boiling water, cover, and steam until the dumplings are tender but still chewy, about 10 minutes. Transfer the dumplings to a warmed platter and serve immediately, accompanied by chili sauce or the Szechuan Peppercorn Oil.

Shiitake Siu Mai

YIELD: 6 TO 8 SERVINGS • ACTIVE TIME: 45 MINUTES • TOTAL TIME: 1½ HOURS

This sweet-and-savory filling will satisfy even the dim sum purist who feels the flavor provided by the pork is essential.

INGREDIENTS

8 shiitake mushroom caps, minced

4 scallions, trimmed and sliced thin

¼ red bell pepper, seeded and minced

¼ cup raisins

¼ cup pine nuts, toasted

¼ cup canned corn

1 tablespoon soy sauce, plus more for serving

1 tablespoon Shaoxing rice wine or dry Sherry

1 teaspoon fish sauce

1 teaspoon toasted sesame oil

2 teaspoons cornstarch

½ teaspoon sugar

½ teaspoon white pepper

36 round Wonton Wrappers (see page 50)

Cabbage leaves, for steaming

Carrots, peeled and minced, for garnish

1 Place all of the ingredients, except for the wrappers, cabbage leaves, and carrots, in a mixing bowl and stir until well combined.

2 Place a wrapper in a cupped hand and fill it with enough of the mixture to fill the wrapper to the top. Flatten the filling with a butter knife and gently tighten the wrapper around the filling, forming a rough cylindrical shape with a flat bottom. Place the filled dumplings on a parchment-lined baking sheet and repeat with the remaining wrappers and filling.

3 Place 1" of water in a large pot and bring it to a boil. Line a steaming tray with the cabbage leaves and then add the siu mai, leaving ½" between each of the dumplings and also between the dumplings and the edge of the tray. Place the steaming tray over the boiling water, cover, and steam until the dumplings are cooked through, tender, and still chewy, about 10 minutes. Transfer the cooked dumplings to a warmed platter, garnish with the carrots, and serve with additional soy sauce.

Zucchini & Shiitake Jiaozi

YIELD: 4 SERVINGS • ACTIVE TIME: 1½ HOURS • TOTAL TIME: 2½ HOURS

Since their shape resembles an early form of currency in China, these dumplings are thought to promise wealth and longevity in Chinese culture.

INGREDIENTS

4 zucchini (about 1½ lbs.), grated

1½ teaspoons kosher salt, plus more to taste

2 tablespoons peanut oil

4 large eggs, lightly beaten

8 shiitake mushroom caps, minced

2" piece of fresh ginger, minced

3 tablespoons soy sauce

3 tablespoons Shaoxing rice wine or dry Sherry

2 tablespoons toasted sesame oil

1 teaspoon black pepper

½ tablespoon sugar

5 scallions, trimmed and sliced thin

40 Basic Dumpling Wrappers (see page 49)

Cabbage leaves, for steaming

Cilantro Chutney (see sidebar), for serving

1 Place the zucchini in a bowl, add the salt, and stir to combine. Let the mixture stand for 1 hour. Working in batches, place the zucchini in a kitchen towel and wring the towel to remove as much moisture as possible. Transfer the zucchini to a large bowl and set aside.

2 Place the peanut oil in a large skillet and warm over medium-high heat. When the oil starts to shimmer, add the eggs and cook, while stirring continuously, until they just set. Transfer to a plate, cut into very small pieces, and add to the zucchini. Add the mushrooms, ginger, soy sauce, rice wine or Sherry, sesame oil, pepper, sugar, and scallions, stir to combine, and season with salt. Place a small piece of the mixture in the skillet, fry until cooked through, and taste. Adjust the seasoning if necessary.

3 Place a wrapper in a cupped hand and place about 1 tablespoon of the filling in the center, making sure to leave about ¾" of the open wrapper around the edge. Moisten the edge with a wet finger, fold into a half-moon, and press on the edge to seal. Place the filled dumpling on a parchment-lined baking sheet and repeat with the remaining wrappers and filling.

4 Place 1" of water in a saucepan and bring it to a boil. Line a steaming tray with the cabbage leaves and place the dumplings in the tray, leaving ½" between each dumpling and also between the dumplings and the edge of the tray. Place the tray over the boiling water, cover, and steam until the dumplings are tender but still chewy, about 8 minutes. Transfer the dumplings to a warmed platter and serve immediately, accompanied by the Cilantro Chutney.

Cilantro Chutney

INGREDIENTS

- 1 bunch of cilantro
- ¼ cup grated fresh coconut
- 15 mint leaves
- 1 tablespoon seeded and minced jalapeño pepper
- 1 garlic clove
- 1 teaspoon minced ginger
- 1 plum tomato, concasse (see page 91)
- 1 tablespoon fresh lemon juice
- Water, as needed
- Salt, to taste

Place all of the ingredients, except for the water and salt, in a food processor and puree until smooth, adding water as needed to get the desired consistency. Season with salt and refrigerate until ready to serve.

Tofu-Filled Momos

YIELD: 4 TO 6 SERVINGS • ACTIVE TIME: 1 HOUR • TOTAL TIME: 1 HOUR

Pressed tofu, also known as dry bean curd, has a dry, compact texture that lends itself wonderfully to these vegetarian dumplings.

INGREDIENTS

8 shiitake mushroom caps

Salt, to taste

½ lb. pressed tofu, diced

2 cups baby spinach

5 scallion whites, diced

2 handfuls of cilantro leaves

3 garlic cloves, minced

2" piece of ginger, minced

2 carrots, peeled and grated

3 tablespoons soy sauce

Basic Dumpling Wrappers (see page 49)

Cabbage leaves, for steaming

Tomato & Sesame Dipping Sauce (see sidebar), for serving

1 Place the mushrooms, a pinch of salt, tofu, spinach, scallion whites, and cilantro in a food processor and pulse until minced and combined. Add the garlic and ginger, pulse to incorporate, and transfer the mixture to a mixing bowl. Add the carrots and soy sauce and work the mixture with your hands until well combined. Place a small amount of the mixture in a skillet, cook it through, and taste. Adjust seasoning if necessary.

2 Place a wrapper in a cupped hand and place about 1 tablespoon of filling in the center, leaving about ¾" of open wrapper around the edge. Moisten the edge with a wet finger, fold into a half-moon, and press down to seal, trying to remove as much air as possible. To pleat the sealed edge, make small folds in the wrapper and press them flat as you work along the edge. Place the sealed dumpling on a parchment-lined baking sheet and repeat with the remaining wrappers and filling.

3 Place 1" of water in a large pot and bring it to a boil. Line a steaming tray with the cabbage leaves and then add the momos in batches, leaving ½" between each of the dumplings and also between the dumplings and the edge of the tray. Place the steaming tray over the boiling water, cover, and steam until the dumplings have puffed up slightly and become slightly translucent, about 8 minutes. Transfer to a warmed plate, tent loosely with foil to keep warm, and cook the remaining dumplings. Serve immediately with the Tomato & Sesame Dipping Sauce.

Tomato & Sesame Dipping Sauce

INGREDIENTS

- 1 tablespoon toasted sesame oil
- 1 tablespoon peanut oil
- 1 small red onion, diced
- 2 garlic cloves, diced
- ½ teaspoon red pepper flakes
- ¼ teaspoon chili powder
- Salt and pepper, to taste
- 3 very ripe plum tomatoes, concasse (see page 91)
- ¼ cup water
- 1½ tablespoons soy sauce
- 2 tablespoons rice vinegar

1 Place the oils in a small saucepan and warm over medium heat. Add the onion, garlic, red pepper flakes, chili powder, and a pinch of salt and cook until the onion starts to soften, about 6 minutes. Add the tomatoes, water, and soy sauce, bring to a boil, and then reduce the heat to medium-low. Simmer until the tomatoes are soft and the sauce has thickened, about 15 minutes.

2 Stir in the vinegar, season with pepper, and transfer the mixture to a food processor or blender. Puree until smooth, place the sauce in a bowl, and let cool to room temperature.

Kimchi Mandu

YIELD: 4 SERVINGS • ACTIVE TIME: 1 HOUR • TOTAL TIME: 1½ HOURS

Each bite of these delicious dumplings proves salty, sour, savory, spicy, crunchy, and creamy.

INGREDIENTS

1 lb. extra-firm tofu, drained and cubed

1½ cups mung bean sprouts, picked over

1½ cups Kimchi (see page 115)

5 garlic cloves, minced

2 large shallots, minced

1 large egg

1½ teaspoons toasted sesame oil

2 teaspoons kosher salt

Black pepper, to taste

Basic Dumpling Wrappers (see page 49)

Peanut oil, for frying

Water, as needed

Sweet & Spicy Dipping Sauce (see page 103), for serving

1 Place the tofu in a single layer on a paper-towel lined baking sheet. Cover with paper towels and pat dry. Let them sit for 30 minutes, changing the paper towels after 15 minutes. After 30 minutes, mince the tofu and place it in a large mixing bowl.

2 While the tofu drains, bring water to a boil in a saucepan. Place the bean sprouts in a bowl of cold water, discard the hulls that float to the top, and rinse under cold water. Add the sprouts to the boiling water and cook for 2 minutes. Remove with a strainer and run them under cold water. Drain, mince, and place in the mixing bowl with the minced tofu. Place the Kimchi in a kitchen towel and wring the towel to remove as much liquid as possible. Mince and add to the mixing bowl. Add the garlic, shallots, egg, sesame oil, salt, and pepper and stir until combined.

3 Place 1 generous tablespoon of filling in the middle of a wrapper. Moisten the wrapper's edge with a wet finger, fold into a half-moon, and press down on the edge to seal the dumpling, making sure to remove as much air as possible. Place the filled mandu on a parchment-lined baking sheet and repeat with the remaining wrappers and filling.

4 Place a large skillet over medium-high heat and add enough oil to coat the bottom. When the oil starts to shimmer, add the mandu in batches and cook until the bottoms are crisp and golden brown, 2 to 3 minutes. Reduce the heat to medium-low, add 2 tablespoons water, cover the skillet, and cook until the water has evaporated. Transfer the mandu to a warmed platter and tent loosely with foil to keep warm. Repeat with the remaining mandu. When all of the dumplings have been cooked, serve alongside the Sweet & Spicy Dipping Sauce.

Tiropitakia

YIELD: 4 TO 6 SERVINGS • ACTIVE TIME: 45 MINUTES
TOTAL TIME: 1 HOUR AND 15 MINUTES

You can make the dough for this Greek delicacy yourself, but the number of quality phyllo options at the store make it okay to take the easy road.

INGREDIENTS

½ lb. feta cheese

1 cup grated kefalotyri cheese, grated

¼ cup chopped parsley

2 eggs, beaten

Pepper, to taste

1 (1 lb.) package of frozen phyllo dough, thawed

2 sticks of unsalted butter, melted

1 Place the feta cheese in a mixing bowl and break it up with a fork. Add the kefalotyri, parsley, eggs, and pepper and stir to combine. Set the mixture aside.

2 Place 1 sheet of the phyllo dough on a large sheet of parchment paper. Gently brush the sheet with some of the melted butter, place another sheet on top, and brush this with the butter. Cut the phyllo dough into 2" strips, place 1 teaspoon of the filling at the end of the strip closest to you, and fold over one corner to make a triangle. Fold the strip up until the filling is completely covered. Repeat with the remaining sheets of phyllo dough and filling.

3 Preheat the oven to 350°F. Place the filled triangles on a buttered baking sheet and bake in the oven until golden brown, about 15 minutes. Remove and let cool briefly before serving.

Potato Pierogi

YIELD: 4 SERVINGS • ACTIVE TIME: 2 HOURS • TOTAL TIME: 3 HOURS

These pillowy treats are as comforting as a rainy spring day spent in a warm bed.

INGREDIENTS

3 Yukon Gold potatoes, peeled and chopped

1 large egg, at room temperature, lightly beaten

4 tablespoons unsalted butter

3 yellow onions, diced

Salt and pepper, to taste

4 oz. farmer's cheese or cottage cheese

1¼ teaspoons sweet paprika

Pierogi Wrappers (see page 61)

All-purpose flour, for dusting

Sour cream, for serving

1 Bring a large pot of salted water to a boil. Add the potatoes and cook until fork-tender, about 20 minutes. Drain, place them in a mixing bowl, and mash until smooth. Add the egg and stir to combine. Set the mixture aside.

2 Melt the butter in a large skillet over medium-low heat. When the butter starts to foam, add the onions, season with salt, and cook until completely soft, about 10 minutes. Raise the heat to medium and cook, while stirring occasionally, until they have browned, about 10 minutes. Remove from heat, let cool for 15 minutes, and then add to the potato mixture. Add the cheese and sweet paprika, stir to incorporate, and season with salt and pepper. Let the mixture cool completely.

3 Place the wrappers on a flour-dusted work surface, place 2 teaspoons of the filling in the center of a wrapper, and moisten the edge of the wrapper with a wet finger. Fold into a half-moon and press down on the edge to seal the pierogi, making sure to remove as much air as possible. Place the filled pierogi on a parchment-lined baking sheet and repeat with the remaining wrappers and filling. When all of the pierogi have been filled, let them sit for 30 minutes.

4 Bring a large pot of salted water to a boil. Working in batches, use a spoon to lower the pierogi into the water. Stir to prevent sticking, reduce the heat to medium, and cook until the pierogi float to the surface, 3 to 4 minutes. Cook for another minute and transfer to a colander to drain. When all of the pierogi have been cooked, serve with the sour cream.

Vegetarian Empanadas

YIELD: 4 SERVINGS • ACTIVE TIME: 45 MINUTES
TOTAL TIME: 1 HOUR AND 15 MINUTES

Achiote is a vibrant orange-red spice that is made from ground annatto seeds, and its nutty, sweet, and earthy flavor is the key to these delectable pockets.

INGREDIENTS

2 teaspoons vegetable oil, plus more for frying

1 yellow onion, minced

1 cup shredded Napa cabbage

2 carrots, peeled and grated

1 garlic clove, minced

1 (14 oz.) can of diced tomatoes

½ teaspoon kosher salt

¼ teaspoon black pepper

½ teaspoon achiote

½ teaspoon cumin

Chili powder, to taste

Dough from Empanadas (see page 150), made with butter

1 Place the vegetable oil in a skillet and warm over medium heat. Add the onion, cabbage, and carrots and cook until soft, about 10 minutes. Add the garlic, cook for 2 minutes, and then transfer the mixture to a mixing bowl. Add the tomatoes and seasonings, stir to combine, and let the mixture cool completely.

2 Add vegetable oil to a Dutch oven until it is 2" deep and bring it to 350°F. Preheat the oven to 200°F and place a platter in the oven. Place the dough on a flour-dusted work surface and roll each piece into a 5" circle. Place 3 tablespoons of the filling in the center of a circle, brush the edge with water, and fold into a half-moon. Press down on the edge to seal the empanada tight, trying to remove as much air as possible. Repeat with the remaining pieces of dough and filling.

3 Working in two batches, place the empanadas in the hot oil and fry until golden brown, about 5 minutes. Drain on paper towels and place them in the warm oven while you cook the next batch.

Soups

Soup is perhaps the only category of food that has dumplings beat in terms of providing comfort and in the number of cultures who take pride in their own unique iterations. That said, it stands to reason that combining the two would result in preparations whose ability to nourish the body and soul is unsurpassed.

With several vibrant variations on the classic wonton soup, a stew that pairs buttermilk's irresistible tang with delicate spinach dumplings, and a spicy, deep-fried take on the iconic combination of grilled cheese and tomato soup, the recipes in this chapter prove that the marriage of these two foods is nothing short of miraculous.

Lobster Wonton Soup

YIELD: 4 SERVINGS • ACTIVE TIME: 20 MINUTES • TOTAL TIME: 20 MINUTES

Lobster and this Thai-inflected broth are ideal for those cold fall days when you're pining for summer.

INGREDIENTS

1 tablespoon sesame oil

1 tablespoon red curry paste

2 teaspoons sugar

3 tablespoons fish sauce

1 (14 oz.) can of coconut milk

Juice of 1 lime

Salt and pepper, to taste

Lobster Wontons (see page 104), cooked

Bird's eye chili peppers, seeded and sliced, for garnish

Cilantro, chopped, for garnish

1 Place the sesame oil in a saucepan and warm over low heat. Add the curry paste and cook, while stirring constantly, for 5 minutes. Add the sugar, fish sauce, and coconut milk to the saucepan and cook, while stirring constantly, for 4 minutes. Add the lime juice and season with salt and pepper. Stir to combine and remove the pan from heat.

2 Divide the wontons between the serving bowls, ladle the broth over them, and garnish with the bird's eye chili peppers and cilantro.

Chicken Stock

INGREDIENTS

7 lbs. chicken bones, rinsed

4 cups chopped onions

2 cups peeled and chopped carrots

2 cups chopped celery

3 garlic cloves, crushed

3 sprigs of thyme

1 teaspoon black peppercorns

1 bay leaf

1 Place the chicken bones in a stockpot and cover with cold water. Bring to a simmer over medium-high heat and use a ladle to skim off any impurities that float to the top. Add the vegetables, garlic, thyme, peppercorns, and bay leaf, reduce the heat to low, and simmer for 5 hours, while skimming to remove any impurities that rise to the top.

2 Strain, allow to cool slightly, and transfer to the refrigerator. Leave uncovered and allow to cool completely. Remove layer of fat and cover. You will have about 8 cups of stock, which will keep in the refrigerator for 3 to 5 days.

Gyoza Soup

YIELD: 4 TO 6 SERVINGS • ACTIVE TIME: 30 MINUTES • TOTAL TIME: 45 MINUTES

Flanking these pale dumplings with bok choy and sugar snap peas makes for a beautiful bowl.

INGREDIENTS

6 cups Chicken Stock (see sidebar)

Salt and pepper, to taste

1 carrot, peeled and sliced thin

Leaves from 4 bok choy

24 sugar snap peas

Pork & Shiitake Gyoza (see page 108)

Scallion greens, sliced thin, for garnish

Edible flowers, for garnish

1 Place the Chicken Stock in a large saucepan and bring to a boil. Reduce heat so that the stock simmers, season with salt and pepper, and add the carrot and bok choy leaves. Cook for 3 minutes and then add the sugar snap peas. Cook until all of the vegetables are tender, about 3 minutes. Remove the vegetables with a slotted spoon and divide them between the serving bowls.

2 Bring the stock back to a simmer. Add the gyoza in two batches. Cook each batch for 8 minutes, remove, and divide between the serving bowls. When all the gyoza have been cooked, ladle 1 cup of broth into each bowl and garnish with the scallion greens and edible flowers.

Seafood Wonton Soup

YIELD: 4 SERVINGS • ACTIVE TIME: 20 MINUTES • TOTAL TIME: 35 MINUTES

The rich, homemade stock makes all the difference in this mouthwatering soup.

INGREDIENTS

1 tablespoon sesame oil

1 yellow onion, minced

2 carrots, peeled and minced

2 garlic cloves, minced

1 cup sake

4 cups Fish Stock (see sidebar)

1 lemongrass stalk, smashed

1 tablespoon soy sauce

1 tablespoon fish sauce

Salt and pepper, to taste

12 Seafood Salad Wontons (see page 106)

1 romaine lettuce leaf, shredded, for garnish

Toasted sesame seeds, for garnish

Cilantro, chopped, for garnish

Radish, shaved, for garnish

1 Place the sesame oil in a large saucepan and warm over medium heat. Add the onion and carrots and cook until they start to soften, about 5 minutes. Add the garlic, cook for 2 minutes, and then add the sake, stock, lemongrass stalk, soy sauce, and fish sauce. Simmer for 10 minutes, remove the lemongrass stalk, and season with salt and pepper.

2 Raise the heat to medium-high and bring the soup to a boil. Add the wontons, reduce the heat to a simmer, and cook until the wontons float to the top, about 5 minutes. Remove the wontons and divide them between the serving bowls. Ladle the broth over the wontons and garnish with the lettuce, sesame seeds, cilantro, and radish.

Fish Stock

INGREDIENTS

½ cup vegetable oil

1 leek, trimmed, well rinsed, and chopped

1 large yellow onion, unpeeled, root cleaned, and chopped

2 large carrots, peeled and chopped

1 celery stalk with leaves, chopped

1½ lbs. whitefish bodies

4 sprigs of parsley

3 sprigs of thyme

2 bay leaves

1 teaspoon black peppercorns

1 teaspoon kosher salt

8 cups water

1 Place the vegetable oil in a stockpot and warm over low heat. Add the vegetables and cook until the liquid they released has evaporated. Add the whitefish bodies, the aromatics, the salt, and the water to the pot, raise the heat to high, and bring to a boil. Reduce heat so that the stock simmers and cook for 3 hours, while skimming any impurities from the surface.

2 Strain the stock through a fine sieve and place in the refrigerator to chill. When the stock is completely cool, remove the fat layer from the top and discard. Use immediately, refrigerate for 3 to 5 days, or freeze for up to 3 months.

Buttermilk Stew

YIELD: 6 TO 8 SERVINGS • ACTIVE TIME: 15 MINUTES • TOTAL TIME: 30 MINUTES

As with many Indian-inspired recipes, there are a lot of ingredients, but don't be daunted—the final result is well worth it.

INGREDIENTS

For the Stew

8 cups buttermilk
½ cup chickpea flour
1 tablespoon turmeric
1 teaspoon kosher salt
1 tablespoon vegetable oil
1 teaspoon coriander seeds
1 tablespoon black mustard seeds
2 large yellow onions, sliced into thin half-moons
6 garlic cloves, minced
2 tablespoons minced ginger
1 teaspoon amchoor powder
2 serrano peppers, seeded and minced

For the Dumplings

2 cups spinach, cooked, drained, and chopped
2 green serrano peppers, seeded and minced (optional)
2 teaspoons kosher salt
1 teaspoon red pepper flakes
1½ teaspoons chaat masala
1 cup chickpea flour

1 Place half of the buttermilk, the chickpea flour, turmeric, and salt in a blender and puree until smooth. Set the mixture aside.

2 Place the vegetable oil in a cast-iron Dutch oven and warm over high heat. When the oil is shimmering, add the coriander and mustard seeds and cook, while stirring, until they start to pop. Reduce the heat to medium and add the onions, garlic, ginger, amchoor, and chili peppers. Sauté until slightly browned and then pour in the buttermilk mixture. Add the remaining buttermilk, reduce the heat so that the stew gently simmers, and prepare the dumplings.

3 To prepare the dumplings, place the spinach, serrano peppers (if using), salt, red pepper flakes, and chaat masala in a mixing bowl and stir to combine. Add the chickpea flour and stir to incorporate. The dough should be quite stiff. Add tablespoons of the dough to the stew. When all of the dumplings have been added, cover the Dutch oven and cook for 10 minutes over low heat. Ladle into warmed bowls and serve.

Stuffed Matzo Ball Soup

YIELD: 4 SERVINGS • ACTIVE TIME: 10 MINUTES • TOTAL TIME: 30 MINUTES

A perfect example of the rewards that can be reaped by thinking outside the box when making dumplings.

INGREDIENTS

1 tablespoon vegetable oil

½ yellow onion, minced

1 carrot, peeled and minced

1 celery stalk, minced

Leaves from 1 sprig thyme, chopped

4 cups Chicken Stock (see page 182)

Salt and pepper, to taste

8 Stuffed Matzo Balls (see page 139)

Parsley, chopped, for garnish

1 Place the oil in a large saucepan and warm over medium heat. When the oil starts to shimmer, add the onion and cook until it starts to soften, about 5 minutes. Add the remaining vegetables and cook until tender. Add the thyme and stock, bring to a boil, and then reduce the heat so that the soup simmers. Simmer for 20 minutes.

2 Season the soup with salt and pepper and return to a boil. Add the Stuffed Matzo Balls and cook until they are warmed through, about 4 minutes. Place two matzo balls in each bowl, ladle the broth over them, and garnish with the parsley.

Penicillin Soup

YIELD: 8 SERVINGS • ACTIVE TIME: 1 HOUR • TOTAL TIME: 4½ HOURS

If you're sick or stuck in bed, this soup is guaranteed to bring a smile to your face.

INGREDIENTS

For the Stock

1 tablespoon olive oil

5 lbs. skin-on, bone-in chicken thighs, trimmed

Salt and pepper, to taste

12 chicken necks (or 4 chicken feet), trimmed

4 chicken backs, trimmed

3 celery stalks

2 carrots, peeled and cut into large pieces

1 leek, trimmed, rinsed well, and cut into pieces

1 yellow onion, halved

3 garlic cloves, smashed and peel left on

12 cups water

Handful of fresh parsley

2 bay leaves

3 tablespoons tomato paste

10 black peppercorns

For the Soup

Reserved cooked chicken meat

5 carrots, peeled and chopped

5 celery stalks, chopped

Salt and pepper, to taste

16 Matzo Balls (see page 36)

For Garnish

Dill, chopped

1 To prepare the stock, place the olive oil in a stockpot and warm over medium heat. As the oil heats up, season half of the chicken thighs with salt and pepper. When the oil starts to shimmer, add them to the pan, skin-side down. Reduce the heat slightly so the thighs gently sizzle and cook for 5 minutes without moving them. Flip and cook the other side for another 5 minutes. Transfer the thighs to a platter. Repeat with the remaining thighs, chicken necks, and chicken backs.

2 Add the vegetables and garlic to the pot and cook until browned, 12 to 15 minutes. Add ½ cup of the water and scrape up the browned bits from the bottom of the pot. Return the chicken pieces to the pot and add the remaining water, parsley, bay leaves, tomato paste, and peppercorns. Stir to combine, bring to a boil, and then reduce the heat to a simmer. Use a wide spoon to skim off the foam that rises to the surface. Cook until the stock is very flavorful, about 3 hours. Remove from heat and let cool. Once cooled, strain the stock into another stockpot through a fine sieve. Separate the cooked chicken meat from the bones, shred it, and set it aside.

3 To prepare the soup, bring the stock to a gentle boil over medium heat. Add the shredded chicken, carrots, and celery. Stir to combine and cook until the carrots and celery are tender, about 15 minutes. Season to taste and divide the Matzo Balls between the serving bowls. Ladle the soup into the bowls, garnish with the dill, and serve.

Ricotta Dumplings in Broth

YIELD: 8 SERVINGS • ACTIVE TIME: 30 MINUTES • TOTAL TIME: 3 HOURS

A celebration of the ricotta dumplings that are near and dear to the inhabitants of Calabria, a region in southwest Italy.

INGREDIENTS

1¼ cups whole milk ricotta cheese

⅓ cup bread crumbs

2 large eggs, at room temperature

1 cup all-purpose flour

¼ cup grated Parmesan cheese

¼ cup grated Pecorino Sardo cheese

2 handfuls of fresh parsley, chopped, plus more for garnish

Salt and white pepper, to taste

10 cups chicken broth

1 Line a fine sieve with cheesecloth and add the ricotta. Place it over a bowl in the refrigerator and let the ricotta drain for 2 hours. After 2 hours, wring the cheesecloth to remove any remaining moisture and place the ricotta in a large mixing bowl. Add the bread crumbs, eggs, ¼ cup of the flour, the remaining cheeses, the parsley, salt, and pepper and stir until well combined. Cover and refrigerate for 30 minutes.

2 Remove the ricotta mixture from the refrigerator and place the remaining flour in a bowl. Roll tablespoons of the ricotta mixture into balls, toss the balls in the flour to coat, tap to remove any excess, and place the balls on a parchment-lined baking sheet.

3 Place the chicken broth in a stockpot and bring to a boil over medium-high heat. Reduce the heat to low so that it simmers and use a spoon to carefully lower the dumplings into the stock. Cook until they float to the surface, 3 to 4 minutes, ladle the dumplings and the soup into warmed bowls, and garnish with additional parsley.

Spicy Dumpling Soup

YIELD: 4 SERVINGS • ACTIVE TIME: 30 MINUTES • TOTAL TIME: 1 HOUR

Invigorating a traditional chicken broth with some spicy dumplings is the ultimate in comfort cooking.

INGREDIENTS

1 tablespoon vegetable oil

½ yellow onion, minced

1 carrot, peeled and minced

1 celery stalk, minced

Leaves from 1 sprig of thyme, chopped

4 cups Chicken Stock (see page 182)

Salt and pepper, to taste

Spiced Dumplings (see page 45)

Parsley, chopped, for garnish

1 Place the oil in a medium saucepan and warm over medium heat. Add the onion and cook until it starts to soften, about 5 minutes. Add the carrot and celery and cook until tender.

2 Add the thyme and the stock and bring to a boil. Reduce heat so that the soup simmers and cook for 20 minutes. Season with salt and pepper, add the Spiced Dumplings, stir, and cook until they are warmed through, about 1 minute. Ladle into warmed bowls and garnish with the parsley.

Creamy Turkey Dumpling Soup

YIELD: 4 SERVINGS • ACTIVE TIME: 45 MINUTES
TOTAL TIME: 1 HOUR AND 15 MINUTES

These dumplings are a great way to use up any turkey that is left over after Thanksgiving dinner.

INGREDIENTS

For the Broth

2 tablespoons vegetable oil

1 yellow onion, chopped

2 celery stalks, chopped

1 celeriac, peeled and chopped

2 parsnips, peeled and chopped

Leaves from 1 sprig of rosemary, chopped

½ cup white wine

4 cups Chicken Stock (see page 182)

1 cup heavy cream

Salt and pepper, to taste

For the Dumplings

4 slices of bread, chopped

½ cup parsley leaves, chopped

1¼ cups all-purpose flour

1 teaspoon baking powder

½ cup whole milk

1 egg

4 tablespoons unsalted butter, melted

1 cup cooked and chopped turkey leg meat

Salt and pepper, to taste

4 cups Chicken Stock

1 To prepare the broth, place the oil in a saucepan and warm over medium heat. Add the onion, celery, celeriac, and parsnips and cook until tender, about 10 minutes. Add the rosemary, cook for 2 minutes, and then add the white wine and stock. Bring to a boil, reduce heat to a simmer, and cook until the vegetables are very tender, about 30 minutes. Transfer the broth to a food processor, puree until smooth, and strain through a fine sieve. Set the broth aside.

2 To prepare the dumplings, place the bread and parsley in a food processor and pulse until combined. Add the flour and baking powder and blitz to incorporate.

With the food processor running on low, slowly incorporate the milk, egg, and butter. Add the turkey to the work bowl and fold to incorporate. Season with salt and pepper, then place the stock in a saucepan and bring to a boil over medium-high heat. Drop tablespoons of the dumpling mixture into the stock, cover, and cook for 12 minutes. Transfer the cooked dumplings to a colander.

3 Add the cream to the broth, season with salt and pepper, and then add the dumplings. Cook until everything is warmed through and ladle the dumplings and the soup into warmed bowls.

Tomato Soup with Spicy Hush Puppies

YIELD: 4 SERVINGS • ACTIVE TIME: 40 MINUTES • TOTAL TIME: 1 HOUR

A fresh spin on the classic grilled cheese-and-tomato soup combo.

INGREDIENTS

For the Soup

2 tablespoons unsalted butter

1 yellow onion, chopped

2 lbs. tomatoes, chopped

2 carrots, peeled and chopped

5 cups Chicken Stock (see page 182)

2 tablespoons chopped parsley

½ teaspoon minced fresh thyme leaves

6 tablespoons heavy cream

Salt and pepper, to taste

For the Hush Puppies

Vegetable oil, for frying

½ cup cornmeal

3½ tablespoons all-purpose flour

4½ tablespoons sugar

¾ teaspoon kosher salt

¼ teaspoon baking powder

⅛ teaspoon baking soda

Pinch of cayenne pepper, or to taste

¼ cup buttermilk

1 egg, beaten

2 tablespoons seeded and minced jalapeño pepper

¾ cup grated Fontina cheese

1 To prepare the soup, place the butter in a large saucepan and melt over medium heat. Add the onion and cook until it starts to soften, about 5 minutes. Add the tomatoes, carrots, stock, parsley, thyme, and cream, reduce heat, and simmer until the vegetables are tender, about 20 minutes. Transfer the soup to a food processor, puree until smooth, and strain through a fine sieve. Set the soup aside.

2 To prepare the hush puppies, add oil to a Dutch oven until it is 2" deep and bring to 320°F. As the oil warms up, place the cornmeal, flour, sugar, salt, baking powder, baking soda, and cayenne pepper in a small bowl and whisk until combined. Place the buttermilk, egg, and jalapeño in a separate bowl and whisk to combine. Add the wet mixture to the dry mixture and stir to combine. Add the cheese and fold to incorporate. Drop tablespoons of the batter into the hot oil and fry until golden brown. Remove and set on a paper towel-lined plate to drain.

3 Place the pureed soup back in the saucepan and warm over medium heat. Season to taste. When it is warmed through, ladle into warmed bowls and either serve the hush puppies on the side or place them directly into the soup.

Desserts

There is something inherently sweet about the term dumpling. It conjures images of warmth, contentment, and happiness by capitalizing on a trope that storytellers have successfully mined for years: that an unassuming exterior is often hiding something unique and lovely. The prospect that something ordinary could contain a surprise is always tempting, as the worldwide love for dumplings bears out.

That said, it should come as no surprise that we saved some of the very best for last. From the Japanese Tang Yuan Dango (see page 202)—which is given a berry-based twist here—to the Galuste Cu Prune (see page 209) that is as photogenic as it is appetizing, these desserts fully represent the joy that dumplings bring people around the world.

Tang Yuan Dango

YIELD: 4 TO 6 SERVINGS • ACTIVE TIME: 30 MINUTES • TOTAL TIME: 2 HOURS

Topping these sweet rice dumplings with freeze-dried berries adds a burst of color and flavor.

INGREDIENTS

4 cups fresh strawberries, hulled and chopped

1¼ cups sugar

1½ cups sweet rice flour (glutinous rice flour), plus more as needed

⅓ cup water, plus more as needed

2 tablespoons canola oil

6 wooden skewers

Freeze-dried strawberries, for garnish

1 Place the strawberries and sugar in a glass mixing bowl and stir to combine. Place 1" of water in a small saucepan and bring it to a boil. Cover the bowl with plastic wrap, place it over the saucepan, and let cook for 1 hour. Check the water level every 15 minutes and add more if it has evaporated. After 1 hour, turn off the heat and let the mixture cool. When cool, strain and discard the solids.

2 Bring water to a boil in a large pot. Place the flour, water, and ¾ cup of the strawberry syrup in a large mixing bowl and use a fork to work the mixture until combined and very dry. Remove 2-tablespoon portions of the mixture and roll each into a ball. Place the balls in the boiling water and cook until they float to the surface and double in size, about 5 minutes. Return the balls to the mixture, add the canola oil, and use a fork to incorporate.

3 Bring the water back to a boil and prepare an ice water bath. Place the mixture on a work surface and knead until it is a smooth and slightly tacky dough. If the dough is too dry or too sticky, incorporate water or flour as needed. Divide the dough into 18 pieces, roll them into balls, and use a slotted spoon to gently lower them into the pot. Gently stir to keep them from sticking to the bottom and then cook until they float to the surface and double in size, about 8 minutes. Remove with a slotted spoon, refresh in the ice water bath, drain, and place 3 balls on each of the skewers. Garnish with the freeze-dried strawberries and drizzle some of the remaining syrup over the top.

Jian Dui

YIELD: 4 SERVINGS • ACTIVE TIME: 1 HOUR • TOTAL TIME: 1 HOUR

One of the most beloved Asian sweet dumplings, red bean paste is another popular filling for these crispy and chewy balls.

INGREDIENTS

¼ cup roasted peanuts, chopped

2½ tablespoons granulated sugar

⅛ teaspoon kosher salt

2 cups sweet rice flour (glutinous rice flour), plus more for dusting

¾ cup water

⅔ cup packed light brown sugar

Peanut oil, for frying

⅓ cup sesame seeds

1 Place the peanuts, granulated sugar, and salt in a food processor and pulse until ground. Be careful not to process the mixture too much and make peanut butter. Place the mixture in a small bowl and set aside. Place the sweet rice flour in a separate bowl and make a well in the center. Place the water in a small pot and bring it to a boil. Add the brown sugar to the pot, stir until dissolved, and then pour the mixture into the well. Stir until a ball of dough forms. Transfer the dough to a flour-dusted work surface and knead until smooth. The dough needs to be hot, so be careful.

2 Cut the dough into 2 pieces and roll each one into a log. The dough tends to dry out quickly, so keep a bowl of water near the work surface and dip your hands into it as necessary. Cut each log into eight pieces and roll each piece into a ball. Cover the pieces with plastic wrap to keep them from drying out.

3 Place a ball in the palm of one hand and use the thumb of your free hand to make a hole in the center of the ball. Fill with 1 teaspoon of the peanut mixture and smooth the dough over the filling. Pinch the seam and twist to remove any excess dough. Roll into a smooth ball, place on a parchment-lined baking sheet, and cover with plastic wrap. Repeat with the remaining balls and filling.

4 Add peanut oil to a Dutch oven until it is 2” deep and bring to 350°F over medium heat. Place the sesame seeds in a small bowl. Dip each ball into the bowl of water, shake to remove any excess, and roll them in the sesame seeds until coated. Working in batches of four, drop the dumplings into the hot oil and cook, while gently stirring initially, until they float to the surface, about 3 minutes. Push the dumplings to the edge of the Dutch oven and baste them with the hot oil as they cook. Cook for another 3 to 4 minutes and transfer to a paper-towel lined plate. Serving the dumplings warm is preferred, but they are also delicious at room temperature.

Luqaimat

YIELD: 4 SERVINGS • ACTIVE TIME: 30 MINUTES • TOTAL TIME: 1½ HOURS

This sweet and simple dumpling is typically served at the end of a fast during Ramadan.

INGREDIENTS

1 cup all-purpose flour

½ teaspoon instant yeast

½ cup nonfat dry milk powder

2 tablespoons sugar

½ teaspoon ground cardamom

Pinch of saffron

⅓ cup lukewarm water (90°F), plus more as needed

Vegetable oil, for frying

½ cup date syrup or honey

1 tablespoon sesame seeds, toasted

1 Place the flour, yeast, milk powder, sugar, cardamom, and saffron in a mixing bowl and stir until well combined. While working the mixture with your hands, gradually incorporate the water until a dough forms. Cover with a dry kitchen towel and rest for 1 hour.

2 Add vegetable oil to a Dutch oven until it is 2" deep and bring it to 350°F over medium heat. Wet your hands and roll tablespoons of the dough into balls. Drop them into the hot oil and fry, while stirring, until they are dark brown, about 3 to 5 minutes. Transfer to a paper towel-lined plate to drain and cool.

3 When all of the dumplings have been cooked, place them in a serving bowl and add the date syrup or honey and the toasted sesame seeds. Toss to coat and serve immediately.

Galuste Cu Prune

YIELD: 4 SERVINGS • ACTIVE TIME: 30 MINUTES • TOTAL TIME: 1 HOUR

As beautiful as it is delicious, this dessert dumpling is the pride of Romania.

INGREDIENTS

3 plums, pitted and quartered

3 tablespoons confectioners' sugar

1½ lbs. Yukon Gold potatoes, peeled and chopped

2 eggs

1 cup all-purpose flour

3 tablespoons semolina flour

¼ teaspoon kosher salt

1 tablespoon olive oil

3 tablespoons unsalted butter

2 cups bread crumbs

6 tablespoons granulated sugar

1 Place the plums in a small bowl, sprinkle the confectioners' sugar on top, and toss to combine. Set aside. Place the potatoes in a saucepan, cover with water, and bring to a boil. Cook until they are fork-tender, drain, and place them in a large mixing bowl. Mash until smooth, add the eggs, flours, and salt and stir until the dough just holds together.

2 Bring water to a boil in a large saucepan and add the olive oil. Place the butter in a skillet and melt over medium heat. Add the bread crumbs, reduce the heat to low, and cook, while stirring frequently, until the bread crumbs are golden brown. Remove from heat, add the granulated sugar, and stir to combine. Let the mixture cool completely.

3 Divide the dough into 12 pieces and flatten them to ¼" thick. Place one of the sugar-coated plums in the center of each piece, shape the dough around the plum, and gently roll into a ball. Place the dumplings in the boiling water and cook until they rise to the surface, about 4 minutes. Remove them with a strainer and roll them in the bread crumbs until completely coated. Place the dumplings on a platter and let cool completely before serving.

Blueberry Varenyky

YIELD: 6 TO 8 SERVINGS • ACTIVE TIME: 1 HOUR • TOTAL TIME: 1½ HOURS

These just may supplant blueberry pie as the reason you eagerly anticipate berry season.

INGREDIENTS

3½ cups fresh blueberries

1 tablespoon sugar

Zest of 1 lemon

Pierogi Wrappers (see page 61)

Salt, to taste

1 tablespoon vegetable oil

5 tablespoons unsalted butter, melted

Confectioners' sugar, for dusting

1 Place two-thirds of the blueberries in a medium saucepan. Add the sugar and lemon zest and stir to combine. Cook over medium heat, while stirring occasionally, until the blueberries burst and release their juice, about 4 minutes. Reduce the heat to low and simmer until the mixture is very thick, about 18 minutes. Stir in the remaining blueberries, remove the pan from heat, and let cool completely.

2 When the blueberry mixture has cooled, place a wrapper in a slightly cupped hand and place 2 teaspoons of the filling in the center. Moisten the edge of the wrapper with a wet finger, fold into a half-moon, and pinch the edge to seal it tight, while trying to remove as much air as possible. Reserve any leftover filling.

3 Bring a large pot of salted water to a boil. Once it's boiling, add the vegetable oil and stir. Working in batches, add the varenyky to the water and stir for 1 minute to keep them from sticking to the bottom. After the dumplings float to the surface, cook for another 3 minutes. Remove the varenyky from the water using a large slotted spoon and shake them gently to remove any excess water. Transfer to a warmed platter, top with some of the melted butter, and gently toss. Tent loosely with aluminum foil to keep them warm while you cook the remaining dumplings. To serve, dust the varenyky with the confectioners' sugar and top with any remaining filling.

Chocolate & Hazelnut Pockets

YIELD: 6 TO 8 SERVINGS • ACTIVE TIME: 45 MINUTES • TOTAL TIME: 45 MINUTES

You won't believe how much better this homemade chocolate-and-hazelnut spread is than what's available at the store.

INGREDIENTS

2 cups hazelnuts, toasted

⅓ cup granulated sugar

1 teaspoon kosher salt

1 lb. semisweet chocolate chips, melted

1 stick of unsalted butter

1 cup heavy cream

36 round Wonton Wrappers (see page 50)

Vegetable oil, for frying

Confectioners' sugar, for dusting

Cinnamon, for dusting

1 Place the toasted hazelnuts, granulated sugar, and salt in a food processor and blitz until the mixture is a paste. Place the melted chocolate, the butter, and the cream in a mixing bowl and whisk to combine. Add the hazelnut paste and stir until incorporated.

2 Place a wrapper in a slightly cupped hand and place 1 teaspoon of the hazelnut-and-chocolate mixture in the center. Moisten the edge of the wrapper with a wet finger, fold into a half-moon, and pinch the edge to seal it tight, while trying to remove as much air as possible.

3 Add vegetable oil to a Dutch oven until it is 2" deep and bring it to 350°F. Working in batches of three or four, add the dumplings and fry, while turning, until golden brown. Transfer the cooked dumplings to a paper towel-lined wire rack and dust with the confectioners' sugar and cinnamon. When all of the dumplings have been cooked, let them cool slightly before serving.

Sweet Semolina Dumplings

YIELD: 8 SERVINGS • ACTIVE TIME: 40 MINUTES • TOTAL TIME: 24 HOURS

Native to northern Italy's Piedmont region, this crispy wonder is traditionally served during Carnevale, a celebration that closely resembles New Orleans' Mardi Gras.

INGREDIENTS

1 tablespoon olive oil

Zest of 2 lemons, cut into thick strips

4 cups whole milk

⅓ tablespoon sugar

¼ teaspoon kosher salt

1 cup semolina flour

1½ cups bread crumbs

2 tablespoons unsalted butter

Grapeseed oil, for frying

3 large eggs

1 Line a 9 x 13-inch baking dish with parchment paper and brush the parchment with the olive oil. Place the lemon zest, milk, sugar, and salt in a saucepan and bring to a boil over medium-high heat while stirring constantly. Strain to remove the lemon zest, return the mixture to the saucepan, and cook over medium heat. While stirring continuously, add the semolina flour to the saucepan in a steady stream. Cook, while continuing to stir, until the mixture is creamy but firm, about 9 minutes. Remove from heat and stir for a few minutes to help the mixture cool. Pour the mixture into the prepared baking dish and use a rubber spatula to distribute it evenly. Let cool to room temperature, cover, and place in the refrigerator overnight.

2 About 1 hour before you are ready to fry the dumplings, remove the semolina mixture from the refrigerator and let it come to room temperature. Carefully invert the semolina mixture onto a cutting board and remove the parchment. Cut into similarly sized diamonds and place the bread crumbs in a wide, shallow dish.

3 Place the butter in a large skillet and add enough grapeseed oil to coat the bottom. Warm over medium-high heat. Place the eggs in a bowl and beat until well combined. Dip the diamonds into the beaten egg, gently dredge them in the bread crumbs until completely coated, and then place them in the skillet. Fry until golden brown, about 2 minutes, and then turn over and cook until golden brown on the other side, another 1 to 2 minutes. Place the cooked dumplings on a paper towel-lined plate to drain and serve immediately once all of them have been cooked.

Gnocchi with Raspberry Sauce

YIELD: 6 SERVINGS • ACTIVE TIME: 1 HOUR • TOTAL TIME: 1½ HOURS

Adding mascarpone and lemon zest lightens the dough just enough to make this gnocchi the perfect end to any meal.

INGREDIENTS

For the Gnocchi

½ lb. Yukon Gold potatoes, peeled and chopped

½ cup all-purpose flour, plus more for dusting

3 tablespoons mascarpone cheese

1 egg yolk

1 teaspoon lemon zest

Salt, to taste

4 tablespoons unsalted butter, melted

For the Sauce

½ cup water

½ cup sugar

½ lb. frozen raspberries

1 To prepare the gnocchi, place the potatoes in a saucepan and cover with water. Bring to a boil and cook until fork-tender, about 10 minutes. Drain, transfer to a large bowl, and mash until smooth. Let the mashed potatoes cool completely. When the potatoes have cooled enough to handle, add the remaining ingredients and work the mixture with your hands until the dough holds together and is no longer sticky.

2 Place a handful of dough on a flour-dusted work surface and roll it into a ¾" thick rope with your hands. Repeat with the remaining dough. Cut the ropes into ½" pieces and roll the gnocchi over the tines of a fork (or a gnocchi board) while gently pressing down to create ridges. Place the shaped gnocchi on a parchment-lined baking sheet and lightly dust them with flour.

3 Bring a large pot of salted water to a boil and prepare the sauce. Place all of the ingredients in a small saucepan and cook, while stirring constantly, until the sugar has dissolved and the mixture has thickened. Remove from heat, strain through a fine sieve, and set aside.

4 Working in batches of 20 gnocchi, add them to the boiling water and stir so that they do not stick to the bottom. When they float to the top, cook for another minute, remove with a strainer, and shake to remove excess moisture. Place the cooked gnocchi in a large bowl, toss with some of the melted butter, and tent the bowl with foil to keep warm. When all of the gnocchi have been cooked, divide the sauce between the serving bowls and place the gnocchi on top.

Pumpkin Pie Wontons

YIELD: 6 TO 8 SERVINGS • ACTIVE TIME: 30 MINUTES • TOTAL TIME: 30 MINUTES

This spin on the holiday favorite is sure to win over even the staunch traditionalists in your family.

INGREDIENTS

1 (14 oz.) can of pumpkin puree (not pumpkin pie filling)

1 (12 oz.) can of evaporated milk

2 eggs, lightly beaten

½ cup sugar

½ teaspoon kosher salt

1 teaspoon cinnamon, plus more for dusting

¼ teaspoon ground ginger

¼ teaspoon ground nutmeg

36 square Wonton Wrappers (see page 50)

Vegetable oil, for frying

1 Place the pumpkin puree, evaporated milk, eggs, sugar, salt, cinnamon, ginger, and nutmeg in a large bowl and stir until well combined.

2 Place about 1 tablespoon of the filling in the middle of a wrapper. Rub the wrapper's edge with a wet finger, bring the corners together, pinch to seal tightly, and transfer to a parchment-lined baking sheet. Repeat with the remaining wrappers and filling.

3 Add vegetable oil to a Dutch oven until it is 2" deep and bring to 325°F over medium heat. Working in batches of six to eight, gently slip the wontons into the hot oil and fry, while turning, until golden all over, about 1 minute per side. Transfer the cooked wontons to a paper towel-lined wire rack and dust with additional cinnamon. Once all of the wontons have been cooked, serve them immediately.

Lemon Curd Samosas

YIELD: 4 SERVINGS • ACTIVE TIME: 1 HOUR • TOTAL TIME: 1½ HOURS

The bright flavor and color of lemon makes it a natural partner for the gorgeous golden burnish of the samosa.

INGREDIENTS

½ cup fresh lemon juice, plus 1 tablespoon

1 tablespoon lemon zest

3 large eggs

1 cup sugar

2 sticks of unsalted butter

Dough for Samosa Wrappers (see page 57)

Maida flour, for dusting

Vegetable oil, for frying

1 Place the ½ cup of lemon juice, 2 teaspoons of the lemon zest, the eggs, sugar, and butter in the mixing bowl of a stand mixer fitted with the paddle attachment. Beat on medium speed until well combined. Pour the mixture into a saucepan and cook over low heat until it is thick enough to coat the back of a spoon, about 10 minutes. Pour the lemon curd into a serving dish, place in the refrigerator, and chill until it thickens further, about 20 minutes.

2 Add the remaining lemon juice and lemon zest to the dough and stir to incorporate. Divide the dough into 8 pieces and roll each one out into a 6" circle on a flour-dusted work surface. Cut the circles in half and brush the flat edge of each one with water. Fold one corner of the flat edge toward the other to make a cone and then pinch to seal.

3 Add vegetable oil to a Dutch oven until it is 2" deep and bring it to 325°F over medium heat. Fill each cone one-third of the way with the lemon curd, moisten the edge of the opening with a wet finger, and pinch to seal. Place the sealed samosas on a parchment-lined baking sheet.

4 Add the samosas to the hot oil in batches and fry, while stirring and turning them over occasionally, until they are golden brown, about 5 minutes. Transfer the cooked samosas to a paper towel-lined plate and let cool slightly before serving.

Index

Metric Equivalents

Weights

1 ounce	28 grams
2 ounces	57 grams
4 ounces (¼ pound)	113 grams
8 ounces (½ pound)	227 grams
16 ounces (1 pound)	454 grams

Volume Measures

⅛ teaspoon		0.6 ml
¼ teaspoon		1.23 ml
½ teaspoon		2.5 ml
1 teaspoon		5 ml
1 tablespoon (3 teaspoons)	½ fluid ounce	15 ml
2 tablespoons	1 fluid ounce	29.5 ml
¼ cup (4 tablespoons)	2 fluid ounces	59 ml
⅓ cup (5⅓ tablespoons)	2.7 fluid ounces	80 ml
½ cup (8 tablespoons)	4 fluid ounces	120 ml
⅔ cup (10⅔ tablespoons)	5.4 fluid ounces	160 ml
¾ cup (12 tablespoons)	6 fluid ounces	180 ml
1 cup (16 tablespoons)	8 fluid ounces	240 ml

Temperature Equivalents

°F	°C	Gas Mark
225	110	¼
250	130	½
275	140	1
300	150	2
325	170	3
350	180	4
375	190	5
400	200	6
425	220	7
450	230	8
475	240	9
500	250	10

Length Measures

1⁄16-inch	1.6 mm
⅛-inch	3 mm
¼-inch	6.35 mm
½-inch	1.25 cm
¾-inch	2 cm
1-inch	2.5 cm

ABOUT CIDER MILL PRESS BOOK PUBLISHERS

Good ideas ripen with time. From seed to harvest, Cider Mill Press brings fine reading, information, and entertainment together between the covers of its creatively crafted books. Our Cider Mill bears fruit twice a year, publishing a new crop of titles each spring and fall.

CIDER MILL PRESS

BOOK PUBLISHERS

"Where Good Books Are Ready for Press"
501 Nelson Place
Nashville, Tennessee 37214

cidermillpress.com